W9-BXT-212

Six Presidents from the Empire State

Six Presidents
from
the Empire State

Edited by Harry J. Sievers, S. J.

SLEEPY HOLLOW RESTORATIONS

TARRYTOWN · NEW YORK

Library of Congress Cataloging in Publication Data
Main entry under title:
Six Presidents from the Empire State.
Bibliography: p.
1. Presidents—United States—Biography.
2. United States—Politics and government—19th century—
Addresses, essays, lectures.
3. United States—Politics and government—1901–1953—
Addresses, essays, lectures.
I. Sievers, Harry Joseph, 1920–ed.
II. Sleepy Hollow Restorations, Tarrytown, N. Y.
III. Title.
E176.1.S59   973'.0992 *[B]*
ISBN 0-912882-07-7

Sept. 18, 1975
74-951

ISBN 0-912882-07-7
Library of Congress Catalog Card Number: 74-951
Printed in the United States of America
First Printing

CONTENTS

ILLUSTRATIONS

Portraits of Presidents Van Buren, Fillmore, Arthur, Cleveland and Theodore Roosevelt are reproduced from the collections of the Library of Congress. The portrait of President Franklin D. Roosevelt is from the Franklin D. Roosevelt Library, Hyde Park, New York.
Appreciation is gratefully acknowledged.

vii

PREFACE

ALL White House incumbents evoke interest, simply because all Presidents make history, some more than others. Indeed, Presidents who come from the same state seem to enjoy a special niche in Clio's closet. Students as well as others can enumerate members of the Virginia dynasty inaugurated by Washington and concluded by Monroe. Others praise Ohio as the cradle of Presidents. The Empire State has a similar claim to fame.

Plans for the publication of this book were made by Sleepy Hollow Restorations as part of its educational service to the academic community and to the general public. Sleepy Hollow Restorations sponsors occasional conferences in various aspects of American history and culture as part of an on-going program. One such conference was held in Tarrytown, N.Y. on September 15 and 16, 1972. At that conference, attended by some two hundred scholars, a consensus emerged that not merely in a presidential election year but long after, interest in the six Presidents who were sent to the White House from New York and in their impact on the presidency would remain high.

The group handily divides itself into three pairs whose terms in office correspond broadly to three major eras in our history—Martin Van Buren and Millard Fillmore, incumbents before the Civil War; Chester A. Arthur and Grover Cleveland, political flowers in the Gilded Age; and Theodore Roosevelt and Franklin Delano Roosevelt, representatives of the modern presidency for nearly a quarter of a century.

The conference members had voiced satisfaction with the six essays and six commentaries presented orally. It is our hope that this volume will afford an opportunity for many others to gain insights and to share new evaluations of the Six.

This book also contains the address of the conference banquet speaker, Professor Louis W. Koenig, eminent political scientist and authority on the presidency. It appears, after updating by its author, in essay form.

All contributors to this volume have had an opportunity to revise their respective manuscripts with an eye to lasting publication. For their prompt cooperation, our thanks. Their scholarly contributions deserve such plaudits as this volume may receive. Errors are my responsibility—or as a modern President might say, "I am ultimately responsible."

HARRY J. SIEVERS, S.J.
Dean of the Graduate School
Editor

Fordham University
New York

Six Presidents from the Empire State

The Presidency in War and Peace

Louis W. Koenig

Each of the six Empire State Presidents under discussion in this volume made important decisions that did much to determine whether their times were to be characterized by violent conflict, at home and abroad. As Edward Pessen points out in his essay in this volume, the first President to come from New York State, Martin Van Buren, is in many ways the prototype of the peace-oriented President. An artist in consensus politics, possessor of a modulated temperament that contrasted, as day does from night, from that of his combative mentor, Andrew Jackson, Van Buren made key decisions that constrained oncoming crises of war.

Despite strong popular sympathies of the American people with the Canadian rebellion of 1837 and a general outcry for war when the British seized an insurgent vessel in American waters, Van Buren held to a course of peace at great personal political cost, to the point that he and his administration were derided as "tools of Victoria."[1] In 1839, a border dispute between Maine and New Brunswick erupted, again threatening war, but Van Buren, with patience and tact, prevailed for peace. There were other diplomatic crises, and Van Buren coped with them. But he also knew failure. The Seminole war in Florida, that fiercest of Indian wars, inherited from Jackson, dragged on and on, costly in lives and money.

There is an opposite kind of presidency, the one about which contemporary critics speak when they contend that the office has accumulated far too much power over foreign affairs and national security, over questions, therefore, of war and peace. These critics see the presidency as a distorted office, a place

1

where the most momentous decisions are made in privacy and secrecy, with minimum interference by Congress, and with little, if any, manifest regard for public opinion.[2] This is hardly a picture of democratic leadership. The continued engrossment of contemporary Presidents in war-making prompts critics to contend further that peace is undervalued in the Chief Executive's decision-making.

Toward the development of this kind of presidency, Empire State Presidents too have contributed imposingly. Theodore Roosevelt is credited with moving the United States from an isolated inward-looking posture, into the arena of world affairs, as a first-rank participant. Winner of the Nobel Peace Prize, he also demonstrated high capacity for autonomous decision, for subterfuge and mastery; he indeed brought the presidency into a position of primacy in foreign affairs. Lesser successors might fumble and diminish the office's impact, yet Roosevelt's achievement was a benchmark to which the more skilled might always revert.

But the presidency about which contemporary critics complain is more the product of still another New Yorker, indeed another Roosevelt. It is Franklin Roosevelt who is the progenitor of the presidency that is criticized and despaired over in the eras of Lyndon Johnson and Richard Nixon. The methods of Roosevelt suffuse the methods of the later Presidents. The methods of Franklin are more complex, indulged in on a larger scale than the methods of Theodore, and their content was one of greater urgency.

Franklin Roosevelt managed what has come to be regarded as "a good war." But that qualitative status was perceived less clearly and was entertained less widely in his time. Opinion about the war and America's relationship to it was highly divided. Isolationism was a flourishing sentiment; disillusionment about the First World War, fought to make the world "safe for democracy," was strong. Symptoms of divided opinion appeared everywhere. The Selective Service Act was barely renewed by one vote in the House of Representatives, just months before Pearl Harbor. In his race for a third term, Roosevelt was so impressed with the force of isolationist sentiment that he was driven to assure the mothers of America "again, and again, and again" that their sons would not be asked to fight in another foreign war.

In his own sentiments, Roosevelt was fervently pro-Ally, and the Nazi overrunning of France in June 1940 spurred him in his purpose and plan not to allow the Allied cause to sink but to provide it with all possible succor. Yet he faced potent hostile opinion in Congress and the public. In his dilemma, Roosevelt constructed a pattern of presidential action which his successors in the military dilemmas of their own day have followed. Its ingredients were autonomy and secrecy of decision, the *fait accompli*, and the subterfuge. This Roosevelt is very much the fox of James MacGregor Burns' biographical title, *The Lion and the Fox*.

An example or two must suffice. The Lend-Lease Act, vital in making available badly needed economic and military commodities to the Allies, contained a provision reflective of isolationist sentiment, which specified that in conveying Lend-Lease material abroad, U. S. naval convoys were not to be employed. Meanwhile, German U-boats were operating with devastating efficiency and, with the British Navy hard-pressed, American naval vessels were soon protecting Lend-Lease cargoes right across to England, notwithstanding the prohibitions of legislation.

Did not this violate the law, Roosevelt was asked at a news conference. Certainly not, he replied, the naval convoys barred by the Act were out of date, and therefore unthinkable. U. S. naval vessels, he went on, were functioning merely as neutrality patrols, sailing the seas, and giving out information on the location of Axis naval craft, and so on. Subsequently, Roosevelt ordered the Navy to "shoot on sight" any Axis vessel they encountered, and although the United States remained technically a non-belligerent, violent engagements followed. In explanation of these and other moves, Roosevelt announced that all necessary force "short of war" would be used to further American aid to the Allies. This too became a debate over semantics.[3] Thus Roosevelt responded to "a good cause," the Allied cause, with manipulation, deviousness, and the *fait accompli*, and surmounted the barriers of divided opinion until the attack on Pearl Harbor united the country.

Roosevelt's presidential successors have each contributed to the growth of the autonomous presidency, especially the office's last two incumbents, Lyndon Johnson and Richard Nixon. Like Roosevelt, they faced divided domestic opinion over a war, the endlessly frustrating war in Vietnam, and like him, they coped with it by elaborating on the autonomous presidency. Since so much of this is recent history, no detailed review of events is necessary. But it is essential for our purposes to recapitulate several kinds of criticisms that are heard nowadays about this presidency.

One is that its decisions are often impetuous and constitute overreactions by the Chief Executive. These allegations are often heard about the Dominican crisis and the response of the Johnson administration, where what in retrospect proved a minor uprising was responded to heavy-handedly by sending in the Marines. A related criticism is that foreign policy decisions may be the result of presidential pique. The sudden heavy aerial bombardment of North Vietnam at Christmas 1972 following a deadlock in the peace negotiations was perceived by many as having this aspect,[4] while others saw it as necessary to bring North Vietnam back to the peace table. If decision-making becomes highly personalized, even if it is presidential, it sooner or later reflects the less attractive qualities of any incumbent, whoever he may be, and this transpires in some of the more unguarded hours of the decision-maker.

Still other criticisms are heard. One is that the decisions of the autonomous presidency are excessively casual, particularly in the light of their enormous importance, whether for the world, the American nation, or their possible political costs to the President himself. During the Johnson years, for example, an institution thrived which contributed significantly to decision-making, and which became known as the Tuesday lunch. This was a gathering of the President with his principal national security aides, typically, the Secretary of State, the Secretary of Defense, his Assistant for National Security Affairs, and one or two others for whom the day's business had special concern. Although the luncheon's purpose was serious, its manner was quite casual in the sense that there was no prepared agenda. Some have suggested that the most planned aspect of the meetings was the menu.

The use of the luncheon for decision development meant that the range of consultation was apt to be narrow, and that it dealt cavalierly with the bureaucracies which had important stakes in its determinations. Not only were these bureaucracies in effect barred from making inputs of advice based upon their unparalleled knowledge and skills, but the responsibility for carrying out the decisions fell heavily upon them.

Then there is the criticism that in its *modus operandi* the autonomous presidency is antithetical to democratic norms and values. Instead of openness and public discussion, it utilizes secrecy and manipulation.[5] Most flagrant of all were the clandestine bombing raids by B-52s in Cambodia in 1969 and 1970, with no disclosure to the public or to Congress while they were in progress and which, in fact, were obscured by falsified statistics reported by the Pentagon to Congress in 1971. The first public information about this secret war-making did not seep out until 1973, almost four years after its initiation. In a further variation of the pattern of secrecy, President Nixon made no public explanation of the Christmas 1972 bombings of North Vietnam before, during, or within a reasonable aftermath following their conclusion. His last news conference was in October 1972. Congressional leaders appeared to have fared little better than the general public.[6] The earlier incursions into Cambodia and Laos presented a similar picture. Like Roosevelt and his "neutrality patrols," the Indochina war had its diversionary jargon, which obfuscated more than it explained, to assist in the evasion of congressional restrictions on presidential powers. Only most belatedly did Congress intervene, as it could have at any point in the Indochina war, by setting an absolute cut-off date, August 15, 1973, for the use of funds for United States bombing in Cambodia.

All this leads to an interest in looking more closely into how presidential decisions are made in foreign affairs and national security, and how their technique and quality might be improved through restructurings of their process. If the decision-making of all the Presidents were studied, it might disclose that some, such as Van Buren, follow patterns that are more conducive to the maintenance of peace than others, such as Roosevelt. Likewise, certain patterns of decision-making may be more compatible than others with democratic ideals of public discussion and official accountability. Pursuit of such an inquiry leads also to a consideration of other components of the political system—to Congress, for example, and its capacity to perform better than it has as a restraint on the President as an enforcer of accountability, and as an influence to help make decisions more rational and deliberate and less personal, more prudent, and more oriented to peace as a high-priority value.

CONGRESS

In their despair over the enlargement of presidential power, many critics look hopefully to Congress. They have offered proposals to move power from the executive branch to Congress, or have exhorted Congress to assert itself, to reclaim power, once possessed in a more imposing past, which has been allowed to slide to the executive.

In terms of democratic ideals and a quest for decision processes which better accord with those ideals, Congress has important attractions. It is in the popular legislature that the different strains of thought and interest are represented. Congress is a deliberative body, a forum for discussion, and many of its proceedings, including those that are decisive and final, are open and reported to the public. Congress' multiplicity of opinions contrasts strongly with the more monolithic, more hierarchical executive, whose members are subject to command and control.

Unfortunately, Congress has certain blemishes which are also relevant. Its members are preoccupied with domestic policy and local problems. The local constituency is the congressman's employer, with effective power to hire and fire. What counts with the constituency is the state of the local economy, employment levels, and the availability of federal largess for local expenditure. In contrast to this bread-and-butter politics of the congressman, foreign policy and its issues seem remote and abstruse, matters of minor consequence for his retention of office. Quite understandably, he tends to accord it a low priority among the issues on which he is prepared to be actively engaged.

As well, the historical record is clear, Congress has no distinctly stronger identification with peace than the President. Like his, its record on the choice between war and peace is mixed. For some past wars, Congress was the most potent moving force toward involvement. In the onset of the War of 1812, the War Hawks of the House of Representatives are remembered as the most potent contributors to the assumption of belligerence. In 1898 American entry into the war with Spain was more the work of Congress than of the President.

Even in the contemporary crises, Congress has sometimes committed itself to a violent response sooner than the President. As President Kennedy deliberated on what to do about the Berlin Wall as it was being thrown up, a resolution emanated from the House of Representatives, pledging support to the President for the use of all necessary means, including force, in the situation. Congress also preceded the President in an expression of similar resolve in the Cuban missile crisis. Other times, Congress has joined with the President in an affirmation of commitment to the use of force, as, witness, the Formosa and Lebanon resolutions of the Eisenhower years and the Gulf of Tonkin resolution for the Vietnam war during the Johnson administration.[7]

Notwithstanding its mixed record, Congress has been the launching place of important efforts to check the enlargement and free use of presidential power. In the 1950s, a formidable assault was commenced by congressional conservatives with the Bricker amendment which aimed to curb the President's power respecting treaties and executive agreements. President Eisenhower and Secretary of State Dulles had to invest considerable effort to defeat the amendment in Congress. More recently Senator Fulbright has championed a national commitment resolution looking toward a procedure by which the President would consult with the Senate and secure expressions of its views before entering into any new commitment in international affairs. During the Indochina war, Senators McGovern, Hatfield, Cooper, and Church, and others, initiated proposals to wield the congressional power of appropriations to restrain the President. Generally, these efforts sought to bar the use of funds for the war beyond a specified deadline for military operations in certain specified areas, such as Cambodia, and were repeatedly unsuccessful until 1973. Understandably, Congress is reluctant to face the political unpopularity that termination of funding for war activities would normally engender.

Of a different genre, and formidable on its face, is the War Powers Act of 1973 which requires the President, after committing the armed forces to combat abroad, to report that event to Congress. The combat action must end in 60 days unless Congress authorizes the commitment, or within an additional 30 days if the President certifies it is necessary for safe withdrawal of the forces. But this new law is not without flaw. On its face, it appears to give the President a blank check to initiate combat action anywhere, subject to later congressional review. The Act bears the seeds of future constitutional crisis. Passed over the veto of a President politically weakened by the Watergate crisis, it might be contested in a future presidency of normal strength. International crises often arise from uncertain purpose and unclear communications, conditions that the new law will foster.

There are still other proposals concerning Congress. One, for example, would establish a permanent legislative committee, a quorum of which would always be available in the capital, and therefore it would be at hand for the President to consult whenever a foreign affairs emergency arose. The President would be expected to deliberate with the committee before involving the nation in armed conflict. The committee's continuous presence is intended to overcome an occasional presidential argument that an autonomous executive decision is necessary because Congress happens not to be in session when an emergency arises and, accordingly, consultation is precluded. But for this, as for the other proposals pertaining to Congress, one may expect presidential resentment and resistance with the contention that it encroaches upon executive power. In addition, history provides many instances where presidential "consultation" is merely an announcement of executive action barely before it is taken.

EXECUTIVE DECISION-MAKING

In light of its mixed historic record and the intrinsic difficulties of the proposals just examined, Congress appears neither promising nor reliable as a serious check upon presidential power over war and peace. The inadequacies of Congress spur an inquiry whether there are other means that might be helpful in this quandary of American democracy.

One area that might be fruitfully examined is presidential decision-making. Such a study might encompass all the Presidents in a quest for decision-making patterns, some of which may commend themselves as more conducive to the maintenance of peace and the avoidance of war than others. The most obvious paths lead to Presidents whose decisions in critical situations came down on the side of peace. Presumably, the patterns of this kind of presidential decision-making can be imitated or adapted by present-day Chief Executives.

As the first President, George Washington was confronted with the critical question of war or peace in the French-British war and America's relationship to it. Portions of public opinion wanted the country to go to war on the side of France, others on the side of Britain, but the first President chose resolutely to keep the country neutral. His pattern of decision-making is instructive for contemporary Chief Executives. In securing advice preparatory to decision, Washington followed two basic principles. He saw to it that this advice was representative of the chief options to be considered. The principle was embodied in the two leading figures of his cabinet: Alexander Hamilton whose views were partial to England, and Thomas Jefferson who favored France. Secondly, Washington believed that the rendering of advice and the weighing of alternatives should proceed competitively. The cabinet provided a perfect forum: in it, in Washington's presence, Hamilton and Jefferson argued their cases, each under challenge from his opponent. Thanks to such decision-making processes, Washington's decisions avoided impetuousness, were prudent and well deliberated, and sidestepped the expenditure of the young nation's strength in an avoidable war.[9]

Washington's salutary principles are applicable to the more complex presidency and executive branch of today. Now representation can usefully be seen in functional terms, derived from the fact that many different departments, with their assigned functions, contribute to foreign policy and national security. By their nature, some of these functions should create, in the departments that assert them, a bias for peace. Thus the State Department's function is diplomacy, which presumably commits it to the conduct of international relations in the peaceful ways of negotiation and representation. Various economic departments are engaged in foreign affairs which also have a functional stake in peace. The conduct of trade between nations, which those departments promote, requires mutuality and trust; commerce and credit depend on confidence.

To secure the optimum contributions of different departments requires facilitative structuring, in the sense that Washington's use of the Cabinet suited that purpose. In the contemporary era, the trends of structuring have been running against the ideal of counsel to the President that is competitive and representative. The last three presidential administrations have contributed to this trend. More and more the flow of advice preparatory to presidential decision has centered in a single helper of the President in the White House office, namely, the Assistant for National Security Affairs. In the years from Kennedy to Nixon, this office has had three extremely able incumbents, McGeorge Bundy, Walt W. Rostow, and Henry Kissinger. In addition, President Nixon's reorganization of the National Security Council, announced in his first State of the World Address, contributed to the trend.[10] Nixon's reorganization of the committees of the National Security Council tends to centralize in Kissinger control over the research and evaluation of the options involved in a decision. The reorganization establishes a centralized, hierarchical arrangement for receiving and disposing of the advice of the various functional departmental contributors. Finally, an extraordinary new phase in the concentration of the power of counsel to the President occurred when Kissinger became Secretary of State while simultaneously continuing as Assistant for National Security Affairs. His incumbency of both positions eliminated the possibility of competing advice from the two top offices assisting the President in foreign affairs.

The new pattern of an enhanced role for the Assistant for National Security Affairs is attractive to the President, since it serves to increase his personal control of preparation for decision, and, thanks to the doctrine of executive privilege, it helps to shut out the unwanted intrusions of Congress. The Assistant can more readily plead the necessity for executive privilege than can departmental representatives. And it more easily thwarts any common effort that sometimes springs up between members of Congress and members of the bureaucracy—the tie, for example, between Senator Kenneth Keating of New York and members of the State Department who fed him information of the Soviet missile build-up in Cuba which enabled the Senator to prod the administration toward responding to the situation. An unresolved question for the future is whether Kissinger in his new dual capacity as National Security Assistant and Secretary of State will be induced by the latter role to be more open in dealing with Congress. His initial conduct as Secretary tended toward openness, but the durability of that stance awaits testing by controversial policy issues. At the very least, Kissinger will enjoy a perpetual option to retreat to the walled secrecy of his position as National Security Assistant.

Instead of an Assistant for National Security Affairs in the fashion of Bundy, Rostow, and Kissinger, who weakens independent departmental staff work and overcentralizes in his hands and those of his own staff of the task of a "search" for and evaluation of the options of a developing decision, it might be profitable to consider the possibilities of a Washington-type pattern. The inquiry is encouraged by the practices of the recent presidencies of Truman and Eisenhower. In those administrations, the Assistants to the President for National Security Affairs were, respectively, Sidney Souers and Robert Cutler. By background neither was particularly versed in national security affairs. Souers was a St. Louis businessman and Cutler a Boston banker. From our viewpoint, their lack of background is a cause for celebration.

The modesty of their preparation plus the well-circumscribed design of the original formation of the position of Assistant for National Security Affairs limited Souers and Cutler to far more modest duties than those that evolved for the later incumbents, including Kissinger. Souers and Cutler can be described as custodians or facilitators who helped the operation of the decision-making process, making certain that each relevant departmental source contributed to the development of alternatives that the President might consider. Watchful that the machinery functioned effectively, with its wide reach, they scrupulously abstained from influencing policy or the articulation and selection of alternatives.

Under Bundy, Rostow, and Kissinger, the position of Assistant for National Security Affairs has burst far beyond its earlier modest boundaries, to the point that its three most recent incumbents have become directors or magistrates rather than custodians or facilitators. Under the present, more grandiose, proportions of the position, the National Security Assistant presides at the apex of the decision-development hierarchy. In this scheme, the assistant shapes policy analysis throughout the executive branch, where his word and wish are heeded because of his unique influence with the President. Consequently, as Alexander George has noted, the assistant overcentralizes the functions of the "search" for and the "evaluation" of decisional alternatives, with marked weakening of the independence of staff work. The assistant, in effect, selects the alternatives that are to go before the President, what is to be emphasized, and what is not.[11]

It is submitted that the possibilities of presidential decisions supportive of peace have a better chance of materializing under the custodian or facilitator model than under the magistrate or director model. In the facilitator model, the departments and agencies whose functions tilt them toward a preference for peace would be better assured an access to presidential decision-making than is the case in the director model. In the latter, the State Department and its function of diplomacy as an instrument of peace are subordinated to the Assistant for National Security Affairs and are vulnerable to his adverse decisions. Under the facilitator model, the State Department has a far larger and more assertive role, as the experience of the Truman and Eisenhower administrations and the impact of a Marshall and a Dulles as Secretary of State suggest.

One of the more outstanding applications of the facilitator model was the decision-making in the Cuban missile crisis of 1962, in which President Kennedy skillfully cultivated the contributions of many departments and agencies, by officials of various ranks—assistant secretaries and bureau chiefs as well as Secretaries. Kennedy deftly minimized hierarchy and authority and guarded against disclosing any premature preference for a particular decisional alternative. The missile crisis mirrored the facilitator model and fortunately produced a nonviolent resolution of a horrendous crisis.[12]

To work effectively, the facilitator model requires the maintenance of many delicate conditions. There must be a relatively even distribution of power and influence among the participating departments and agencies, since the undue ascendance of any one participant nullifies the model. There must be an equitable distribution of a number of ingredients: information and analytical resources, skills at bargaining and persuasion, perception and comprehension of the issues. As a *sine qua non*, the President himself must be committed to this model. His supportive behavior, as Kennedy's in the missile crisis suggests, is indispensable. Finally, the use of this model is time-consuming, just as the maintenance of peace is, requiring lengthy, patient exploration of options.[13] Admittedly, a balance of so many factors is itself an element of weakness, but the hope is that it would make presidential decision-making more peace-prone, by enlarging its horizons, and by controlling impetuousness, a trait that often triggers conflict into violence.

INTEREST GROUPS

A search for a better structuring of presidential decision-making, one more prone to peace, leads to a further arena—a large and crowded one in American politics—that of interest groups. Like Congress, interest groups are closely oriented to domestic affairs and less so to foreign affairs. It is in the domestic marketplace that they stand, normally, to gain or lose most on their bread-and-butter concerns. As with Congress, foreign affairs seem remote from the consequential economic and political struggles at home. The absorption of interest groups in domestic affairs and their far less presence in foreign affairs, contributes to a steady phenomenon of American history, the heavy concentration of presidential advisers and helpers in foreign affairs on the East Coast. By the criterion of the numbers of persons in the foreign affairs establishment, all other regions of the country are deprived areas. Characteristically, the leading presidential associates for foreign affairs and national security affairs, whether the administration is Republican or Democratic, are drawn heavily from the Empire State and one of its most historic avenues, Wall Street, and from the Ivy League colleges and universities in the East. All three National Security Assistants discussed in this paper—Bundy, Rostow, and Kissinger—have these characteristics. The impression is fortified by mention of such prominent names of the foreign affairs establishment of late years as Harriman, Forrestal, Dulles, Acheson, Kennan. This geographic concentration violates President George Washington's principle that presidential advisers should possess broad geographic representativeness, so as to articulate different points of view.

Most members of the foreign affairs establishment have little connection or concern with domestic social problems. In orientation, they readily give foreign policy priority superior to that of domestic policy. Except for the later phases of the Vietnam war, they have generally pursued foreign and national security policy on a bipartisan basis, thus removing many of the concerns in those fields from party politics and popular debate.

All this leads to a contention that the prospects of peace in presidential decision-making might be improved if the domestic-oriented interest groups, and especially groups concerned with urban problems and with other urgent social problems, became involved in national security policy-making. The price of their abstention is, as the Vietnam war testifies, that social policy expenditure is given a lowered priority in wartime, as outlays are concentrated on the battlefield.

Consequently, Martin Luther King was correct in seeking to enlist the civil rights movement in the task of bringing the Vietnam war to a conclusion. Likewise, the National Welfare Rights Organization (NWRO) was wise in stressing the importance of ending the war, which was perceived as a barrier to genuine welfare reform.[14] These and other domestic groups, and particularly those concerned with social problems, have a huge stake in the preservation of peace. If they increased the effectiveness of their organizations, and directed more attention to international affairs, they might gain more impact on the president and his counsellors. Peace is too important to be left only to Presidents; it must be worked and struggled for in many quarters of society well beyond the White House.

The Modest Role of Martin Van Buren

Edward Pessen

W HEN I advised a colleague recently that I had been asked to prepare a paper on the impact of Martin Van Buren on the presidency, he remarked that the paper would no doubt be a short one. In those presidential rating games that historians and political scientists love to play, Martin Van Buren does not come off too well. He is not placed in the bottom rank: his intelligence and ability were too high for that. And it is widely believed that the failure of his administration was due primarily to circumstances beyond his power to control—the Panics of 1837 and 1839 and the depression that followed in their wake. Yet typically he is ranked well below not only the great Presidents but the very able and some of the moderately successful Chief Executives as well.[1] Nor is the occasion for the present discussion in any sense a sign of a new, more appreciative perception of the achievement of the eighth President. Van Buren is on our agenda only because he was the first New Yorker to ascend to the nation's highest office. Yet, if my remarks shall indeed be brief, it is due not to the insignificance of Van Buren's tenure so much as to the format of this celebration. Millard Fillmore, Chester A. Arthur, Grover Cleveland, and the two Roosevelts are getting equal time with Old Kinderhook, neither more, nor less.

While the exigencies of space leave me no alternative but to paint in broad strokes, students eager for new hard data should not be disheartened. A modest renaissance of Van Buren scholarship promises in the near future to fill out many of the empty spaces left by the partial and inadequate biographies done earlier by Edward Shepard, Denis Tilden Lynch, and

Holmes Alexander.[2] Not the least of the happy consequences of
the new evaluations being prepared by Robert V. Remini and
Donald B. Cole and the comprehensive edition of the Van Buren
papers being assembled under the direction of Walter L. Ferree
should be the substitution of firmer, contemporary recollections
of events involving Van Buren for the after-the-fact, unavoidably
biased recollections of them he himself left in his *Autobiography*.[3] The latter work is of course marred not only by
its reliance on a memory inescapably grown rusty, but by its
incompleteness—it only carries the story up to the vice-presidency
—and by its partiality. For, as Van Buren admitted in 1854
when he began writing it, his purpose was not to write detached
history but to vindicate his own administration.

Van Buren was astute enough to realize that his reputation
as political wirepuller, sometime dissimulator, and master of evasiveness, stood in the way of his hopes for a successful presidency. Van Buren had not attempted to mask his ambition to
become the President of the United States. With what an un-
critical biographer describes as "pleasing frankness," Van Buren
wrote admirers as he left the highest office that to attain it had
been his "most earnest desire."[4] His entire career prior to 1836
made this amply clear. Van Buren would have been less than
human had he not also yearned for a glorious presidency once he
had achieved his great desire. And he was indeed human.

I find one of the choicest specimens of the famed Van Buren
character and intellect in the comments he made, first on the
eve of advancing to the highest office and later a decade after
he departed from it: comments ostensibly humble and bespeak-
ing Van Buren's admiration of other, greater national leaders;
comments actually critical of the popular judgment for not
sufficiently appreciating a man like Van Buren because, unfortunately, it was a judgment formed more by emotion and prejudice than by reason. Like Napoleon, Van Buren in "retirement"
fought a literary battle for the vindication of his historical reputation. Unlike Bonaparte, however, he fought it unsuccessfully,
in part because he fought it too subtly, primarily because by no
possible exaggeration could Van Buren point to a record of great

victories, and perhaps in part—a very small part, true—because his unkind appraisal of the popular mind may not have been altogether inaccurate.

In his inaugural address on March 4, 1837, Van Buren told the people that he belonged to a "later age" than did the first seven Presidents, all of them in a sense children of the American Revolution. Van Buren was born one year after Yorktown. "I may not expect my countrymen to weigh my actions with the same kind and partial hand," he continued. What were these remarks but an attempt to make excuses in advance, no matter how disarmingly and offhandedly, to show that he, Van Buren, through no fault of his own would be accounted as less than his predecessors even when he performed as well as they? The decisive defeat he suffered at the hands of William Henry Harrison in the 1840 election confirmed his worst fears. In his *Autobiography* Van Buren disingenuously, subtly, but insistently chose to interpret his repudiation by the people as due rather to the deficiencies of the mass intellect than to the deficiencies of the Van Buren administration.

The chief fault of that regime, according to the man variously known as the fox, the wizard, and the magician, was his own too-simple honesty and forthrightness. Alas, such traits morally admirable though they were, doomed their possessor in a complex political world that better rewarded more cynical characteristics. Had he "possessed a tithe of the skill in subtle management and of the spirit of intrigue, so liberally charged upon [him] by [his] opponents . . . [he] could have turned aside the opposition."[5] Particularly fascinating is Van Buren's discussion of the sources of political popularity. What purports to be an explanation of why such a man as his hated political enemy, DeWitt Clinton, was less popular than Jefferson and Jackson, requires no inspired reading to be understood rather as a defense of uncharismatic, unemotional men whose great achievements are undervalued only because the people, bless them, do not know how to think straight.

"In this matter of personal popularity," Van Buren writes, "the working of the public mind is often inscrutable. In one re-

MARTIN VAN BUREN
December 5, 1782–July 24, 1862
The Eighth President of The United States

spect only does it appear to be subject to rule, namely in the application of a closer scrutiny by the People to the motives of
public men than to their actions."[6] What follows makes clear
that Van Buren means *supposed* motives rather than actual ones.
"When one is presented to them possessed of an ardent temperament who adopts their cause, as they think, from sympathy . . .
they return sympathy for sympathy . . . and are always ready to
place the most favorable construction upon his actions. . . . But
when a politician fails to make this impression—when they on
the contrary are *led* [italics mine] to regard him as one who
takes the popular side of public questions from motives of policy, their hearts seem closed against him, they look upon his wisest measures with distrust, and are apt to give him up at the first
adverse turn in his affairs."[7] Which President, one wonders, had
the people been "led" to regard distrustfully, for all the wisdom
of his policies? The people in their wisdom were usually right in
their "discriminations," he continued, as was evidenced by their
quite just preference of Jackson and Jefferson to Clinton. But
they were "sometimes wrong." Modesty no doubt forbade a
more explicit statement, one suggesting perhaps that the most
glaring example of such popular error had occurred in 1840
when a wise leader had been given up at the "first adverse turn
in his affairs."

Posterity has of course judged the Van Buren administration not by the self-serving reminiscences of its chief figure but
by its actions and policies. It must be clear that I am a partisan
neither of Van Buren nor of his great political patron,[8] not least
because of the sycophancy displayed by the former and the
egomania by the latter in their relationship. For example on
learning the "secret" that Van Buren had told Peggy Eaton of all
people, that she was never never to convey to Andrew Jackson:
Van Buren's belief, that is, that Andrew Jackson was the greatest
man who ever lived since he was without fault, Jackson confided
to a then-intimate that Martin Van Buren was a "man without
guile!" The Van Buren record is too liberally sprinkled with
acts of surpassing amorality, the *Autobiography* too much given
to uncorroborated self-loving pronouncements, for my taste. Yet

respect for historical truth requires me to give the magician passing marks, at least for part of his performance. The very fact of a Van Buren administration, after the earlier failures of George Clinton, Aaron Burr, and Daniel Tompkins to realize their hopes of landing presidential nominations, testified to the consummation of one of Van Buren's ambitions—that the state of New York be given "her due weight in the union."

That pragmatic disposition, that preference for conciliation to confrontation no doubt partially explain the low profile assumed by Van Buren's government in dealing with potentially explosive international issues, but they do not detract from the credit his administration rightly earned by its sobriety. Van Buren's policy of evading the increasing clamor for forceful action against Mexico over Texas, Britain over the disputed Maine territory, and Canada over the Caroline affair, contrasts most happily with his predecessor's penchant for fomenting larger crises over smaller provocations. A totally unscrupulous demagogue, serving during the worst economic crisis the nation had yet suffered, could easily have sought his political salvation in the classic manner—by rattling the sword. It is to Van Buren's credit that he never stooped so low. Van Buren's was not "great" foreign policy; many scholars appear to reserve that accolade for the exciting, activist measures associated with the Polk, Wilson, or Truman administrations.[9] If I may paraphrase Brecht, unfortunate is that nation whose leaders pursue great foreign policy. Van Buren's negative achievement in this realm suggests the value to a people of having undoctrinaire opportunism rather than moralistic absolutism at the controls in times of international tension.

The Van Buren record, of course, contains other praiseworthy actions. Richard P. McCormick, who is very far from being a Van Buren enthusiast, notes that under the shadow of almost unremitting Southern skepticism, if not hostility, Van Buren labored skillfully to defuse the terrible issues that divided the sections and would one day tear the Union apart.[10] Donald B. Cole advises me that in reading Van Buren's correspondence he was struck by "the extent to which the Seminole War bothered" Van

Buren.[11] James C. Curtis' recent study reveals other examples of constructive achievement by the Van Buren administration.[12] While I myself do not admire Van Buren's presidency, I do admire the man, in part for his intelligence, even more for his good sense, his personableness, his emotional balance—traits that I regard as significantly positive in the character of a Chief Executive. Time does not permit anything like full treatment. If my assessment of Kinderhook remains essentially a negative one, it is neither because of an animus toward the man nor due to an unwillingness to recognize his positive achievements, but only because the weight of the evidence appears in my subjective judgment to justify such an appraisal.

I have elsewhere suggested that the political skills Van Buren displayed prior to his election to the presidency seemed to desert him after he attained office.[13] That comment should be modified. The skills were still there, as was the intelligence directing them. But tactics that worked so well behind the scenes, whether in Albany or Washington, were not at all certain of success when employed in full public view from the White House. The consummate politician who built the Regency machine, who cemented the North-South alliance and organized the Congressional coalition that in 1828 elected as President a military chieftain of known spleen but unknown political views, who encompassed the destruction of his main rivals for political preferment both in New York and the nation, the man who in the words of his unlikely friend John Randolph "rowed to his object with muffled oars," continued to operate after 1836 as he had done before. Curtis' valuable study of the Van Buren presidency is aptly titled *The Fox at Bay*. Curtis discloses numerous examples of the "magician's" wizardry, whether in purporting to regard William Marcy's lukewarm response to his financial program as though it were enthusiastic approval, or going through the motions of offering to Virginia a cabinet post he knew would be refused, or first making use of and then discarding the brilliant but erratic support given his Independent Treasury or Sub-treasury proposal by John C. Calhoun, or in suggesting that the latter measure, whose chief designer was a conservative Vir-

ginia banker, was somehow a challenge to the forces of aristoc-
racy and wealth. All this was clever. But it may be that in
presidential politics cleverness is not enough or that what is truly
clever is only what pays off.

Van Buren himself and others sympathetic to him believed
that fate played him a dirty trick. For all his desperate attempts
to blame the financial panics and the depression on Nicholas Bid-
dle and the other allegedly aristocratic forces of evil, such as the
unlimited credit system, his administration was unable to free itself of the dread taint that took hold in the popular mind. Now,
the Panic of 1837 was, of course, not caused by anything done
by the Van Buren administration (although many men in and
out of his party thought the policies of the Jackson administration had helped bring on the debacle). Yet it is a fair question:
What did Van Buren do in the face of the crisis? What did he
try to do ?

Curtis tells us and rightly that the idea of a "vast legislative
program," such as was initiated by another New Yorker in the
White House almost one hundred years later, was "alien to [Van
Buren's] day."[14] Van Buren's own belief, expressed to the special session of Congress he had summoned in September 1837,
that "all communities are apt to look to Government for far too
much," was a principle of laissez-faire widely shared in his day.
Clearly his response to the domestic crisis would be a limited
one. It is not ahistorical present-mindedness, however, to ask:
What was the *nature and effectiveness* of Van Buren's response?
For he prepared a most elaborate response and he and his lieutenants professed to put much stock in it. This is not the place
for one more detailed dissection of the Independent Treasury.
Many persons sympathetic to Van Buren have conceded that the
idea of storing federal monies elsewhere than in state banks was
a mouse masquerading as a mountain, its chief supporters motivated above all by narrow considerations of partisan political advantage. It not only took the national government out of the
business of trying to regulate the currency. It was peripheral to
the needs of the army of Americans suffering under the economic dislocations and the appalling maldistribution of wealth

that characterized city and country.[15] For all the fiery rhetoric trumpeting this "bold new policy," in the words of Bray Hammond the policy "subjected banking capitalists to nothing more than being called hard names. Otherwise it was a course to which [bankers] became reconciled . . . and whose termination years later they did not welcome."[16]

The fault of Van Buren was not that he believed that "the wisest course is to confine legislation to as few subjects as is consistent with the well being of a society," but in the dubious judgment he showed in choosing the "few subjects" to be concentrated on. To describe as he did the enactment of the Sub-treasury bill, which he delayed signing until July 4, 1840, four months before the election of 1840, as the "second Declaration of Independence" was not only far-fetched but, even worse, it was stupid. Old Tippecanoe may have been elected for the wrong reasons, his success one more sign of the simplemindedness of the American people. Yet that people are as complex as any other. According to Van Buren, he had been defeated in 1840 "almost without reference to the soundness or unsoundness of [his] principles but thro' the instrumentalities and debaucheries of a political Saturnalia, in which reason and justice had been derided. . . ."[17] Another explanation is possible. In rejecting Martin Van Buren and his party, the people may also have been voting astutely against politicians in this instance both inept and insulting.

Quite apart from his failures as national leader, Van Buren's image as manipulator and trimmer clung to him, clouding over all his presidential policies, offering grist to the propaganda mills of his political opponents. And the legend took. Thus in the Recorder's Court of New Orleans, on October 13, 1840, as reported in *The Picayune*, a worthy citizen complained: "Ven my old voman locks the door and goes out, [our neighbor] makes a fox on it vith chalk and writes underneath it, 'this here is Sly Reynard, from Kinderhook, vot vas for sometime in the London Zoological Gardens, but now is in the Menagerie at Vashington; he is the most cunning hanimal vot's known to naturalists'."[18] It is not necessary to credit the more ridiculous allegations of his detractors about Van Buren's alleged foppishness, cowardice, amorality, and a cunning they said he inherited from his supposed natural father, Aaron Burr, to conclude that to a large extent his reputation was solidly earned. Marvin Meyers has written that the American people could like but not deeply honor men whose fame derived from organized party activity and maneuvering.[19] I trust it does not exalt too much the judgment of the American people to suggest rather that they withhold their deepest admiration from men whose careers are or appear to have been devoid of attachment to great humane principles. Political skill, as informed commentators on the Democratic Roosevelt regularly remind us, is not held against a man. Van Buren was shrewd enough to talk up principles, but his actions appeared to belie his words. For that matter he was frank enough to have stated that his "great" political ends were party unity, punishment of enemies, reward of friends, his own success. As Robert Remini's discerning study of Van Buren's role in creating the new Democratic party made clear,[20] Van Buren's idea of a great Jeffersonian principle was the caucus system of nomination. These were slight goals. It was this real deficiency of heart that largely accounts for Van Buren's small claims to the affection of the American people.

Van Buren and the Uses of Politics

Richard P. McCormick

IN THE INDEX of Edward Pessen's admirable book, *Jacksonian America*, one finds the following key words under the name of Martin Van Buren: demagogy, disingenuousness, evasiveness, inconsistency, opportunism, and shrewdness.

Although with characteristic grace and charity Professor Pessen has muted the severity of these epithets in his admirable essay, he hardly indicates glowing approval of the first New Yorker to make it to the White House. He finds little that was admirable in Van Buren, and I have reason to believe that he is equally unenthusiastic about Jackson, Polk, Pierce, and Buchanan.

I do not propose to undertake the rehabilitation of the Sage of Kinderhook, but I am prepared to argue that we may be blaming him, and his contemporaries, for what were essentially weaknesses inherent in our American political system and in our political culture. The Presidents of the United States in the pre-Civil War decades headed a very imperfect Union, and this consideration severely circumscribed their basic strategies and limited their effectiveness as political leaders. Van Buren, if he is to be fairly evaluated, must be judged within this context. In addition, he must be viewed against the background of the New York political scene, especially in relation to presidential politics.

This collection, if it has made us aware of nothing else, has brought home the fact that prior to the Civil War only two New Yorkers attained the presidency. One of them, the obscure Millard Fillmore, got there by accident. The other, Martin Van Buren, was the designated heir of Andrew Jackson and had served an apprenticeship as Vice-president.

This is not a very impressive record for the Empire State. New York from 1820 on was the most populous state in the Union and had the largest electoral vote. It was also a pivotal state in almost every election. We may assume that New York was not lacking in able men. Why, then, this rather poor showing in the race for the presidency?

It was definitely not due to lack of interest or effort. There were only two elections between 1792 and 1860 when a New Yorker was not on the ticket of some party, as a candidate for either President or Vice-president. No other state matched that record of avidity. It was not lack of effort, any more than lack of political weight as a state, that accounted for New York's indifferent success.

Certainly during the period of the first party system we can attribute the poor showing of New York to the conscious strategy of the Virginians, who cleverly maintained their dominant position in what we call the Virginia-New York alliance. As an element of the Virginia strategy, New Yorkers were relegated to the number two place on the Republican ticket. Thus, for all but twelve years between 1801 and 1837, New Yorkers served in the vice-presidency, a frustratingly insignificant office in those days. I am inclined to give considerable credence to the hypothesis advanced by Jabez Hammond: namely, that it was the deliberate policy of the crafty Virginians to sow sufficient discord among the Republican factions in New York so as to prevent any New Yorker from securing unified support in a bid for the presidency.

Even beyond this shrewd manipulation by the Virginians, we must recognize that there was persistent and general Southern opposition to the choice of any Northern man for the presidency. This Southern antagonism was exhibited against John Adams in 1796 and against his son in 1824 and 1828, and it was to operate against Van Buren in 1832 and after. Not until Pierce, in 1852, was a Northerner to run well in the South, and then only because the Whig Party in the South was tottering on the verge of dissolution. It is an ironic fact that, in spite of his extraordinary commitment to the strategy of building a North-South alliance, Van Buren remained suspect in the South merely because he was a Northerner.

In 1832, for example, when Van Buren was nominated as Jackson's running mate, he fared badly at the hands of Southern delegates to the Democratic National Convention. He received 209 votes, but 49 negative votes were cast by delegates from Maryland, Virginia, North Carolina, South Carolina, Alabama, and Kentucky. In the ensuing election, Jackson-Barbour tickets were run in four Southern states: Virginia, North Carolina, Alabama, and Mississippi, forecasting the opposition that was to mount against Van Buren in the South between 1832 and 1836.

When the Democratic Convention met in 1835 to nominate Van Buren for the presidency, it is significant that there were no delegates in attendance from South Carolina, Alabama, or Tennessee, and a total of only 11 delegates from the states of Mississippi, Georgia, Missouri, Louisiana, and Arkansas. This meager turnout did not indicate enthusiasm for Jackson's designated heir in the South. In that election, although Van Buren eked out a victory, he received less than 50 percent of the popular vote in the South. He lost Georgia and Tennessee, both of which had voted nearly 100 percent for Old Hickory in 1832.

It is difficult to escape the conclusion that Van Buren managed to edge into the presidency in 1836 only because the Whigs had not yet succeeded in developing an effective national organization. He was, in due course, soundly beaten in 1840, losing most of the South. And mainly as a result of Southern opposition he was denied renomination in 1844. Little wonder that his bitterness found expression in 1848 in his candidacy at the head of the Free Soil ticket! The conclusion to be drawn is that it was truly remarkable that Van Buren, a Northerner, managed to attain the presidency in violation of what could be regarded as the norms of American politics in his era.

His success, if we may so label it, was commonly attributed to his mastery of the craft of politics. There would seem to be little dissent from the general verdict that the Old Fox was a master politician. However, this dimension of his career merits further study and reconsideration. Van Buren learned his political skills in a very special school. New York politics in the early part of the nineteenth century was a hard school. I cannot elaborate all of the extraordinary features that distinguished New York politics in those decades, but I would merely suggest that it placed a special premium on deviousness, on shrewdly negotiated but unstable alliances, and on astute manipulation of patronage. It was a politics with a limited popular base, a weak orientation to issues, and constantly shifting factions. Van Buren had, or he acquired, the special skills to succeed in this style of politics.

His greatest achievement as a politician was in welding together the Bucktail Party between 1817 and 1820. By building what was essentially a state-based party, unconnected with national politics, he scored a unique accomplishment. Even more remarkable, he and his associates in the Albany Regency were able to hold the Bucktail Party together despite the treacherous vicissitudes of presidential politics and make of it the stable political organization that controlled the state for two decades. In a state where political loyalty had been conspicuously absent, Van Buren was able to make loyalty to party a supreme value. Using thorough organization, in contrast to the brand of charisma on which DeWitt Clinton had relied, Van Buren and the Regency wrought wonders in constructing their Bucktail-Democratic Party.

Van Buren applied the skills he had acquired in New York to building the Jacksonian coalition and to enhancing his position within Jackson's retinue. But, having recognized these skills and the results they produced, we must be equally cognizant of Van Buren's limitations, which also stemmed from the kind of training he had received in the specialized environment of New York politics.

Van Buren never really adapted to the new politics that came into vogue in the Jackson era. He was a politician's politician, rather than a democratic politician. Recall, for instance, his opposition to universal suffrage in the New York Constitutional Convention of 1821. Or his ill-advised opposition to the popular election of electors in 1824. Or his lasting preference for the caucus system. Van Buren was quite insensitive to the popular style of campaigning that came into vogue in the 1830s and 1840s. For documentation of that insensitivity, consult his 75-page blueprint for the 1840 election campaign in New York. It was a fine blueprint for 1820, but was totally outmoded by 1840.

Van Buren made no contribution whatsoever to the three notable political innovations of the Jackson era. These were the shift to the popular election of presidential electors, the delegate convention system, and the theatrical campaign style. His politics was old-fashioned by 1840. As he puzzled over the forces that had brought about his defeat, he somewhat lamely blamed Whig frauds and popular delusion. Van Buren remained essentially a Jeffersonian in political style as well as in political principles.

Turning, finally, to Van Buren as President, we must concede that he has not been viewed as one of the leading occupants of that office. His tenure is not associated with illustrious achievements. Rather, Van Buren carried the policies of negativism to even greater extremes than his predecessor. The sole monument to his domestic policy was the independent-treasury system, which represented yet a further retreat by the federal government from involvement with the nation's economy. No President ever pursued a milder foreign policy, which earns him his only good marks from Professor Pessen. Over and over again, he voiced his philosophy of state rights and limited government, perhaps nowhere more forcefully than in his message to the special session of Congress in 1837. We can be critical, as is Professor Pessen, of this negativist philosophy, but we are also under some obligation to understand and explain it.

We might start with the proposition that the greatest problem confronting national statesmen in this era was that of holding the Union together. There was a very weak sense of commitment to the national political community, weak support for the national political system. After 1830, there was the additional complication of intensified sectionalism. In the messages of the Presidents, no theme is more constant than the exhortation to preserve the Union. Jackson emphasized this theme in his Farewell Address, echoing the dire forebodings of Washington and forecasting the concerns that were to be voiced with matchless eloquence by Lincoln.

Recognizing the weakness of support for the national political system, and the mounting force of sectionalism, the Jacksonians developed a strategy that represented their solution to the problem of how best to maintain the Union. The essence of that strategy was to remove from the political arena what Jackson frequently referred to as "jarring issues." Thus, the tariff would be compromised. The Bank would be terminated. The issue of internal improvements would be referred back to the states. A gag-rule would be adopted to keep anti-slavery petitions from creating discord in Congress. Texas would be ignored.

Such a policy of negativism raised a crucial problem. How could you persuade the people of the democracy not to make any demands on their government? The answer was to promulgate the dogma that that government was best which governed least. The dogma was made persuasive by the Jacksonian contention that every act of government really favored the rich and the special interests. Such favoritism could be avoided only by adopting a policy of negativism.

Another support for the dogma was the exaltation of free enterprise and reliance on the natural order. By constantly propagating this simple but plausible doctrine, the Jacksonians sought to strengthen cultural inhibitions against recourse to governmental assistance. They made low governmental outputs a virtue. They did this in order to lessen pressures on the imperfect Union.

The discerning Frenchman, Alexis de Tocqueville, saw this strategy and commented on it frequently. One of his observations will suffice to illustrate his perception:

I am strangely mistaken if the federal government is not constantly losing strength, retiring gradually from public affairs

and narrowing the circle of action. It is naturally feeble, but
it now abandons even the appearance of strength.

Van Buren's course becomes more intelligible when we understand it in terms of this strategy of Union maintenance. It
explains why, in his presidential messages, he never referred to
the tariff or to internal improvements. He went to extraordinary
lengths to keep the Texas issue out of politics. He sympathized
with the gag-rule and with the suppression of the distribution
of Abolitionist documents in the South. And in the same vein he
sought to dispose of yet another jarring issue by bringing about
a complete divorce between the federal government and the
banking system, with his independent-treasury system.

What other option did Van Buren have? True, John Quincy
Adams had posed an alternative, recommending to Congress at
the start of his administration a positive program that was to
produce consternation and ridicule, but no action. Later, the new
Republican Party also posed an alternative to the negative strategy of Union maintenance, and the consequence was the disruption of the Union.

As I promised, I have not sought to rehabilitate Van
Buren, or make him out to be greater than he was. But I feel
more sympathy for his predicament than does Professor Pessen.
He was a product of the political culture in which he matured.
And the strategy he pursued in presiding over an imperfect
Union made sense, even if it has failed to command the regard
of latter-day liberal exponents of the positive state.

Millard Fillmore: The Politics of Compromise

Robert J. Rayback

For the most part historians have used little of their special talents to investigate, and then judge, the contributions of Millard Fillmore and his administration in the drama of America's story.[1] Instead, analysts of the mid-nineteenth-century scene have blindly accepted the epitaph for Fillmore which his archenemy, Thurlow Weed, wrote—"A vain and handsome mediocrity!"— as the final appraisal of the man and his work.[2] Having thus billed him as a supernumerary they felt justified in ignoring him with dismissal.

To these reporters it made little difference that during Fillmore's administration the United States thrust itself irreversibly into its historic Oriental orbit. Unconcerned with contradictions, they recognized that, during Fillmore's years for responsibly managing the nation's sovereignty, seismic quakes shook its foundations; yet, somehow under this presidential nonentity, the union survived. Entrapped by a thinking process that accepts trends as the inevitability of "the times," they resort to the passive voice and rarely ask the question: Who made "the times" and how did he or they make them? Those few who have dared to use the active voice accept a litany that others, not Fillmore, were responsible for both the Far Eastern venture and the survival of the federal Union.

Assigning the credit or discredit for these two achievements raises the impossible historical task of measuring the exact weight of factors in the cause of any event. Looked at from the high point of time, however, causes appear only as part of a process, not weights on a balance scale. From this view, only someone with Fillmore's economic outlook and political training

33

could have used the office of the President to bring about results of such magnitude. His contribution to the process was to cast the nation permanently into its Far Eastern role and to provide a method or technique which would become axiomatic in political decision-making.

Past evaluations have missed Fillmore's perceptive recognition that amoral and desperate politicians had artificially emotionalized a significant portion of the nation with alarms over an unreal threat of the extension of slavery into the territories. In consequence of his own insight, Fillmore artfully used the presidential office to restore a more normal fervor to the political process. Historians, however, have tacitly condemned him because he refused to use the alleged opportunity to mount a presidential offensive against slavery. Forgotten in this judgment is his intelligent refusal to drive the nation into a hopeless physical confrontation as a method of eliminating slavery—a goal for which few were morally ready and for which the nation was unprepared.

Fillmore obtained his two abiding convictions—the future material well-being of America could be enhanced by expanding world commerce, and the nation's internal diversity required political accommodations—from his experience in New York State. His local environment taught him lessons of goal and method which he transposed to the national scene. Put another way, Fillmore's presidency relates the story of his community's impact on the nation.

His birth on January 7, 1800, in a log cabin shared by two brothers and their families on the frontier of America's New York wilderness—town of Locke—was no mean force in Fillmore's lifetime outlook. He grew up on the edge of poverty. His father and uncle lost their farm, became unwilling, discouraged tenants, and never succeeded at subsistence farming. With relentless regularity, they, their children, and their neighbors, deserted their isolation and the hostile land of the scenic Finger Lakes region.[3]

Even as Millard Fillmore became a teenager, his family encouraged him to escape the entrapment of the soil. He tried an

MILLARD FILLMORE
January 7, 1800–March 8, 1874
The Thirteenth President of The United States

apprenticeship to a small-time woolens manufacturer, moved to a law clerk's office as a handyboy with an opportunity to "read" law, and eventually followed his father to East Aurora, 20 miles southeast of Buffalo.

It was Buffalo that beckoned him to his future and implanted in him the precepts that continued to guide him.

Buffalo gave Fillmore an unshakable faith in the beneficence of trade and commerce. By 1822, when he moved to Buffalo, its residents had repaired the damage inflicted by the British torch during the War of 1812 and were caught up in a building boom that would continue far into the future. During the previous five years the construction gangs of the Erie Canal had inched their way westward across the state. At Rochester, advance units had built an aqueduct to carry the Canal across the Genesee River, and shortly the pick-and-shovel gangs had arrived in Buffalo. The basins for harboring canal boats were under construction, and offshore barges laden with great stones plied the waters of Lake Erie toward a breakwall that was slowly emerging to make a basin for Great Lakes ships. Already Buffalo possessed over 300 buildings, and its population bordered on 4,000. Speculators scrambled for land, building and hydraulic-power sites, harbor construction contracts and future shipyards. The hum of Buffalo's busy life was unrivaled in almost all the great West.

By 1830, Buffalo was a booming village of about 8,000 people. Most of its hustle and bustle took place less than a mile south of Fillmore's home at a place called "The Dock." This was the wharfed portion of the right bank of Buffalo Creek which the Erie Canal entered and from which it drew water for the eastward flow.

The livelihood of almost all Buffalonians depended on the dock. For at least the first 15 years of its life as the Canal terminal, Buffalo's primary function was to funnel thousands upon thousands of immigrants into the Old West and follow them up with tons of the artifacts of civilization. From this trade the young village mushroomed into a rich, fat city. By 1840 Buffalo's population was pushed beyond 18,000. Eventually the "colonized" West produced products—mainly wheat—for her trade offering to the world, and the wheat trade transformed Buffalo into the nation's milling center and the Erie Canal into the mid-century's wheat carrier par excellence. In consequence, from 1841 when Fillmore became chairman of the House Ways and Means Committee to 1850 when he became President, his home town's population passed 40,000.[4]

In the meantime, at the other end of the Erie Canal–Hudson River waterway, while Fillmore's Buffalo rose from ashes to the nation's nineteenth largest city, merchants changed New York City from one among many to the primary port in the western hemisphere. Thirty-five percent of the nation's exports left through the New York City port, and 65 percent of the nation's imports arrived at New York's wharves. Its population (in that day population growth was the measurement of prosperity) went from 100,000 in 1820 to over one-half million in 1850. During these same years, between New York City and Buffalo, commercial entrepreneurs constructed the pieces of the New York Central railroad trunk line and most of the Erie railroad.[5]

By 1850, New York State had found the role she would play in history—she was one of the world's great throats of commerce—and, by establishing that role, she assured her inhabitants of a livelihood quality that was only a dream a generation earlier when Fillmore fled the farm.

This change of life-style permanently engraved on Fillmore a reverence for this kind of progress. As a young man he had stood in awe-like admiration of commerce's teeming activity, and as an adult he threw himself into the process of nurturing that change from grubbing farming to opulent exchange.

As a lawyer Fillmore drew most of his clients from the commercial world. As a state legislator, he provided the liberating life-style a voice in government through the political parties in New York that were most tender of commercial interests—Antimasonry and its ally, the National Republican Party. As a young state assemblyman, Fillmore's most significant contributions were a bankruptcy law and the elimination of the debtors' prison. These laws freed the businessman of the threat of lifetime indebtedness for a business failure and possible imprisonment until his debt was paid. No one underestimated the force of these acts in opening the way to business ventures.

As a Whig congressman, and ultimately as the chairman of the Ways and Means Committee, Fillmore concerned himself with national banking and its ability to create a wide trading market through a stable, uniform money and credit system. In that day trade within the United States was even more hampered by the "value of the dollar" than it would become more than a century later on the international scene. Fillmore was responsible for the Tariff of 1842, the first really general protective tariff in American history. Fillmore was disgusted at President Polk's veto of the Rivers and Harbors bill of 1845—a measure aimed primarily at improving transportation on the Great Lakes, with its promise of making those lakes an improved extension of the Erie Canal.

When he was Comptroller of the state of New York, Fillmore set about freeing the state banks from political control and made banking a servant of business activity instead of the tool of the surviving elements of the Albany Regency's political machinations.[6]

So universally known was Fillmore's alert attention to the needs of the local business community, it surprised no one when he carried his attitude into the White House and used the presidency for action. He did not view trade as a participant, for he never owned any business, and the closest he ever came to actual promotion arrived much later in his life, when he invested heavily in railroad stocks and bonds. Yet during the debates on the Compromise of 1850, while others were preoccupied with its effect on their individual political lives, he cooperated with Stephen A. Douglas to arrange the first federal land grants for railroad construction in the Mississippi valley. One day federal subsidies would be fraught with favoritism and scandal, but when Fillmore smiled down from presidential heights on trade and commerce, he served no special, venal interests. Rather, his outlook was visionary. Commerce to him was godlike—modern man's chief provider and benefactor—and he honored its leaders and advanced their cause wherever he could.

In 1851, at an elite gathering of state officials and railroad promoters celebrating the completion of a long chain of railroads connecting the Canadas with Massachusetts and commencing a line of steamers between Boston and Liverpool, President Fillmore exuded joy: "I am glad that" Massachusetts "has stretched forth her iron arms to . . . the Canadas. . . . I am entirely in favor of all means by which states and countries can be bound together by the ties of mutual business interests and relations. . . . I rejoice in all measures which . . . strengthen and enlarge our foreign commerce."[7]

Here, whether wishing it or not, Fillmore exposed the bedrock foundation of his foreign policy and virtually promised to use his presidential powers to build a structure on that policy. The results are still visible.

In 1850 the overseas area that beckoned American traders to strengthen their ties and multiply their profits was the Orient.[8] China was no new place for American merchants. Her treasures had long tempted Yankee skippers. Earlier, Fillmore's tariff of 1842 had added its weight to encourage captains to ply the Pacific waters by taxing their competitors at higher rates.

For a long time other countries had tried to open the Orient for their merchantmen, but with the exception of the East Indies, all efforts had failed. British merchants finally acquired access to five Chinese ports as a result of the Opium War of 1842, and the United States soon shared in that opportunity through the Cushing Treaty of 1844. Simultaneously, technological change —the use of steam instead of sail—required national aid for two commerce-enhancing developments. First, the route to the Orient had to be shortened, and secondly, coaling stations had to be located on the highway to the East.

In the 1840s the search for the short route brought the Whig administrations into feverish competition with the British for the primary rights to the isthmian crossings of Central America. Fillmore inherited this foreign policy, and his efforts, like his predecessor's, failed because he refused to use force to help Nicaragua expel the British from Greytown on the Mosquito Coast. But Fillmore's peaceful intercessions left Americans building railroads across the isthmus.

In acquiring coaling stations on the Pacific's main trade route to the East, President Fillmore was more successful. In 1851 his administration persuaded bellicose Napoleon III to abandon his two-year occupation of Honolulu. Hawaii thus became an open way-station for American steamers. Beyond this mid-Pacific refuge, however, stretched numberless miles, sparsely dotted with island havens. None belonged to America, none was fitted out for coaling, but one possessed a coal supply—Japan.

For over 200 years Japan had kept her ports closed to foreign trade. Periodically, enterprising captains had knocked at Japan's door to inquire whether she had changed her mind, and were always rebuffed.

Hitherto the efforts had been half-hearted, but with Fillmore in the Executive Mansion, a virile determination seized Washington. "The moment is near when the last link in the chain of Oceanic steam navigation is to be formed," read the instructions to the first commander chosen to command the squadron to Japan. Steps "should be taken at once to enable our . . . merchants to supply that last link. . . ." It "is desirable that we obtain, from the Emperor of Japan, permission to purchase from his subjects the necessary supplies of coal. . . ."[9]

When Commodore Matthew Perry inherited this charge along with the detailed instructions, he thoroughly understood the purpose of his mission. In July 1853, six months after leaving Norfolk with four warships, he entered the Bay of Yedo. With firm dignity he delivered President Fillmore's address into the hands of the shogun, and in ten days, promising to return, he steamed out of the bay.

Internal conditions in Japan were ideal for such a display of force and restraint. When Perry returned in February 1854, this time with seven ships, Japan's leaders readily signed a treaty including all that Perry asked. Though meager, the concessions revolutionized Japan's former policy. Fillmore had not only prepared the ground for sweeping changes in the relations between the East and the West, but his steamship highway to the Orient was taking shape.

What followed Fillmore's conscious, not accidental, use of presidential power to open the vast Asian market—with resulting benefits to America's livelihood—future events did not dismiss lightly. His was the first government planning to expand trade that bore fruit. Eventually the nation's entire imperialistic venture, not only in the Far East but in the Caribbean region as well, revolved around the axis which Fillmore's administration had begun to spin. Even 120 years later, as rapprochement with Communist China developed, hovering over President Nixon's Peking mission was Fillmore's vision that expanding trade in China could exceed the profits of the Japanese connection.

If earlier Fillmore had contributed his talents to the creation of New York as a throat of commerce between Europe and the developing American West, then, through use of the presidential office, he shaped the practical creation of another throat of commerce between the Orient and the Western world.

The second set of experiences that Fillmore carried into the White House from his intimate knowledge of the New York scene evolved from politics.

In 1820 Fillmore began his political career in a modest manner, casually associated with the National Republican coalition to support John Quincy Adams. By 1828 Fillmore was involved in one of America's earliest political hoaxes: the Anti-Masonic Party.

There was little that was anti-Masonic in the formation of the Anti-Masonic Party except the spicy concoction its creative cooks spoonfed to the voters who showed a liking for the diet. The excitement following William Morgan's disappearance in 1826 was got up for political effect by Thurlow Weed—"the Wizard of the Lobby"—to obtain New York's electoral vote by deception for J. Q. Adams. In this effort Millard Fillmore acted as an eager young man fronting for Weed's machinations on the Erie County scene. Fillmore's reward was nomination and election to the state assembly as an Anti-Mason.[10]

The process by which Fillmore entered the political arena hardly projected him as a man of unquestioned integrity. In the next two elections and during his three terms in the assembly, Fillmore's initial experiences received reenforcements in the great game of American politics. His political actions became a series of backroom coalitions with National Republicans, open wooing of the "Workies" of the Workingmen's Party, and subtle arrangements with Democratic opportunists, and ended, between 1834 and 1836, with Fillmore helping to piece together from many coalitions a mosaic of alliances that became the Whig Party. By the time he moved to Washington as a congressman in 1837, Fillmore was well-versed in American politicking techniques and the role the politician played on the American scene.[11]

If the tergiversations, somersaults, twistings, and turnings portrayed a politician trying—no matter the contradictions of principle—to win control of sovereign power, the portrait was correct. Whether or not Fillmore would be condemned for his methods was, and would be, open to debate. More important for the future, however, the experience taught him lessons and left him with one major precept. The American scene—if it were to be an American scene instead of a Balkanized regionalism—required harmonization of its discordant groups. The responsibility for the task of harmonization belonged to the practitioners of politics.

Fillmore learned at least six lessons about the realities in American politics.[12]

1. The real pulse of action came from local—regional—groups seeking to control sovereignty, or governmental power, for their own ends.

2. Since no single group could hope to obtain sovereign power through its own numerical strength, it must ally or coalesce with other groups who might have the same or different—even conflicting—reasons for wanting to exercise sovereignty.

3. The result of this absolute need for coalition was an ongoing groping search for and experimentation with "bedfellows"— even "strange bedfellows."

4. The experimentation in alliances created state and national

political parties which had no unity of principles, no common goals, no agreement on priorities of achievement, no decalogue of ideals, or no unifying morality.

5. Since no group was willing to admit openly to others—and sometimes not even to itself—that its political goals served crass self-interest, each group, and the coalition as a whole, must justify its appeal for votes on "higher" grounds. Thus, issues that rise above mundane self-interest must be found. The alliance leadership actually looked for issues that could be whipped into a frothy frosting to cover the raw substance of the layer cake. To change the metaphor: the "higher issues" acted as an adhesive —a glue—to hold the pieces together.

6. Once an issue was prepared to give righteous, adhesive decoration to self-interest, disassociating from the issue became extremely difficult. It exposed the pieces for what they were, and unless new cement were quickly applied, the coalition, by falling apart, sacrificed its purpose: control of sovereignty.

These lessons, which Fillmore learned at the beginning of his political life, were reenforced during his congressional years between 1837 and 1843, were used in his gubernatorial campaign in 1844, and dominated the period from his return to politics as the winning state comptroller in 1847 through his months in the vice-presidency.

Thus when he became President on July 10, 1850, Fillmore was prepared to use the lessons of his past experience to achieve exactly their intended use: harmonize discordant elements of the American scene.

The opportunity to apply the lessons came as a challenging crisis—one that threatened the nation's survival—over the nature of the government to be devised for the territory acquired from Mexico. When eventually settled, the crisis ended in a series of measures collectively called the Compromise of 1850. One statute created conventional territorial governments for Utah and New Mexico with the status of slavery to be determined by the residents at the time of admission to statehood. Another defined the boundaries of Texas and reduced her claim by 70,000 square miles. The third admitted California to the Union as a "free" state. The fourth rewrote the Fugitive Slave Act of Washington's first administration. The last abolished the slave trade in the District of Columbia.

The whole controversy,[13] raging in Congress for seven months, had a gestation period of six years and an aftermath of at least three years. It had developed out of politics keyed to the need to create an issue (lesson number five). Fillmore settled it by finding a new adhesive for a coalition (lesson number six).

Back in 1844, some leaders in the Whig coalition, dissatisfied with their lack of success at the national level, began to cast about for other groups to add to their alliance (lesson number two). Some were even willing to replace old groups with new ones. These searchers called for a "new departure,"[14] which was that era's euphemism for lesson number three. They found it in a spinoff of the Mexican War. Before and during the war, Abolitionists had firmly implanted in the political rhetoric the idea that the territorial acquisitions of the war represented a conspiracy of slaveholders to expand their institution into undefiled areas. The Abolitionists through their Liberty Party could not sell the idea to many voters, but unsuccessful Whigs, who previously had scorned the Abolitionists, saw their opportunity to use this appeal, draw Abolitionists into their camp, and then, by watering down Abolitionism to non-extension of slavery into the territories, retain those parts of the Whig coalition controlled by slaveholders and their dependents. Northwestern elements, normally Democratic, interested in free land for homesteads instead of plantations might achieve their goal by switching to the Whig coalition.

At first the Whig slaveholders did not fight the experiment with the "new departure" because they opposed territorial expansion which would create new competitive areas. Southernly located Whig groups, however, soon discovered that their local enemies could and did use this defection from local mores to upset local Whig control (lesson number one). Quickly these Whigs sponsored Zachary Taylor,[15] a Louisiana slaveholding sugar planter and hero of the Mexican War (which Whigs had opposed), and made "heroism" their issue (lesson number six). This issue sought to smother the "new departurists" by removing the need for a "new departure," i.e., by winning the national election with the old coalition (lesson number five).

The strategy almost worked. Taylor, with Fillmore as his running mate, won the election, but, unfortunately for the plan, the Whigs won the presidency only because the Free Soil Party that had emerged for the election of 1848 had caused enough defection in Democratic ranks—notably in New York. But they won neither house of Congress. The Whigs could conclude only that their party, after 16 years of struggling, was still a minority party in the nation. "New departurists" could also see that the Free Soil Party's strength showed that the "free-land, free-soil" issue was a viable one. Thus, those who wanted to broaden the coalition base of the Whig Party consciously set about persuading a number of the original proponents of Taylor, including Taylor himself, to take steps to use the free-soil issue for the party's own future benefit.[16] Their strategy required making the Mexican Cession into states, and giving the appearance that local voters voluntarily chose to keep slavery out of the new states. The plan was soon dubbed the "President's Plan," or "Taylor's Plan."

The strategy backfired. Though the whole issue of extension or non-extension of slavery into the territories had originally been concocted for political use, it was now very difficult to discard it by trying to bypass the question with Taylor's Plan. Southern Whigs discovered it was impossible to stay alive in their own regional bailiwicks by creating states free of slavery. Their local enemies exposed their inconsistency. Yet "new departurists" could not abandon the Taylor Plan because it would lose them their momentum for creating a majority national party. Both sides fretted with anxiety.

Behind the scenes, some Whigs from the South appealed to Taylor and his colleagues to change their tactics, but the "new departurists" were like thirsty horses that smelled water. They had California assured, and they had the method of creating free states out of the rest of the Mexican Cession. Too bad that their old allies to the south were finding it so difficult to adjust. Some, if they dared, might have to leave the coalition.

These Southern Whigs were not about to leave their old, safe home without protest. They fought back by throwing up a barrier to the success of Taylor's Plan—join together the whole question of the future government of the entire Mexican Cession, including California, into one piece of legislation with three parts. They conceived and introduced the Omnibus bill. Now if the "new departurists" wanted a "free" California in the Union, they would have to give up their antislavery plans for the rest of the Cession. The threat that the Executive Office presented to Whigs with Southern constituencies also gave many Democrats cause for concern for their own party's well-being. The administration's scheme for the Cession would strain the North-South axis of the Democratic coalition as it tried to recover from the desertions it had suffered to the Free Soil Party. As early as February 1850, these alarmed congressional Democrats had joined their Whig counterparts in framing the Omnibus bill.[17] As long as it stood untested—and so close was the division in the Senate that no one knew whether it would be passed or defeated—all action to resolve the conundrum came to a halt. All that was heard was the battle of words, and that battle raged until Taylor died and Fillmore became President.

In terms of the story of applying lessons of his past, this was the condition Fillmore inherited.

1. He was well aware of the tangled mess his colleagues had created to meet their needs for present and future goals. He had watched the latest act in the drama from the presiding chair of the Senate. All revolved around deciding how the area acquired from Mexico would be governed. Would the area be created immediately into three states that would be admitted to the Union free of slavery? Or would the residents of the area determine their own condition some time in the future under the precept of "popular sovereignty"?

2. He knew, as most everyone knew, that the possibility of slavery ever going into the territories in question was so remote

that his generation would never have to face a decision. The anti-extension-of-slavery issue was only an adhesive concocted by some of his associates to glue together a winning national coalition for the future.

3. Yet his old coalition still had a chance for future victories if the conveniently manufactured slavery issue for the territories could be quieted and thus make it possible to disengage gracefully from the tussle.

4. If the unnecessary fight did not end, the immediate prospects were for a geographic polarization of politics. There would be a political North and a political South. Never before in the nation's history had this occurred (and it would not until 1860). Considering the federal nature of the Union, such a polarization augured ill for the life of the nation. All the essential props would then be in place for a secession movement.

Essentially Fillmore had to answer the question: On which side should he put the weight of the Chief Executive? On the side of the old coalition that revolved on a North-South axis, or on the side of a new coalition that would revolve on an East-West axis whose units were confined to the North?

Fillmore did not have much time to make up his mind. On the day he took office he discovered that in an area claimed by Texas, the upper reaches of the Rio Grande at Santa Fe, federal troops under orders to hold their position faced hostile Texas troops.[18] Almost simultaneously with receiving this knowledge, the news that Governor Bell of Texas had ordered an additional 2,500 men to the front to stake out Texas' claim alerted the rest of the country to an imminent clash. Something had to be done to untie the Omnibus tangle and reach a political settlement of the border dispute. Otherwise, war between state and federal troops might touch off enough emotional dynamite to make a political settlement impossible. Fillmore acted quickly and, in so doing, answered his fundamental question. He cast his weight on the side of retaining and repairing the old coalition and sacrificing whatever promise others thought the "new departure" held for the future.

Fillmore's answer arose from the first lesson he had learned 22 years earlier: the real pulse of politics came from local-regional groups seeking to control sovereignty for their own ends. With this he mingled another lesson: no group was willing to admit openly to others that its political goals served self-interest and, therefore, it had to justify its appeal on "higher" grounds. The last lesson gave Fillmore the method for making the difficult disassociation from the issue that exacerbated the congressional debate and threatened armed hostilities: apply a new mastic to the joints of the old coalition.

What had made the Omnibus bill unacceptable to a majority of senators was its requirement that each must take the bad with the good, as a significant portion of his constituency defined bad and good. Each senator preferred to be identified only with the interests of his locality. Should the Omnibus be broken into its several parts, each senator could vote for those measures with which he could live at home. An analysis of the positions of each senator's needs promised a majority on each measure. Each majority, however, would be made up of different members. The strategy was useful not only to senators in the Whig coalition, but to those in the Democratic Party as well. The senators in the Democratic coalition were caught up in the same convulsion as their opponents on the other side of the aisle.

Thus, after necessary White House arrangements[19] with Senate and House leaders in both parties to obtain commitments, after stacking the Cabinet with men who symbolized accommodation, and after heroic parliamentary maneuvers, the Senate as committed tore the Omnibus apart on August 3, 1850, 23 days after Fillmore took office. Within a week, the three individual measures of the Omnibus—California, territorial governments for Utah and New Mexico, and the Texas boundary settlement —plus a new Fugitive-Slave Act cleared the Senate. Hesitation developed on the abolition of the slave trade in the District of Columbia, but that jumped its hurdle on September 13. Meanwhile, the House approved each measure as it appeared, and by mid-September Fillmore affixed his signature to each statute.

As if by magic, the storms of contention, which threatened disunion, disappeared.[20] In ten short weeks, Fillmore's administration had solved the problem of territorial government that had plagued the political coalitions since American and Mexican troops first clashed four years earlier. Taken together, these measures were called the Compromise of 1850. Yet, in passing them, no one had compromised.

To call these five laws a "compromise" when they were not held the key to the usefulness of the lessons Fillmore had learned and applied. Coalition politics required that whenever an issue is removed it must be replaced quickly with a new one. Fillmore had an ideal substitute at hand: "Preserve the Union!" By identifying these five measures as a "compromise" to preserve the Union, the less-noble sectional issues could be replaced with a "higher" one. There could be no greater or more laudatory purpose for a coalition of discordant elements than the bedrock reason why harmony was needed: the accommodation of discord for the Union itself.

For the rest of his administration, Fillmore used every written or traditional power of his office to sell the idea that the compromise was a final solution of the issue of slavery in creating national political coalitions. No longer could opportunists use it to cement together another national party; the "higher" issue of the Union must triumph. As a result, his administration imposed a great silence on the issue of slavery as a tool for politicking. In its stead, "finality" and "Union" prevailed.

Eventually unhappy politicians, in their search for a way of creating a winning combination, felt compelled to return to the magic and hazard of the slavery-in-the-territories issue. But that return brought about the consequences that Fillmore had feared: polarized politics, disunion, and civil war.[21]

Fillmore's performance in this crisis period of American history has been portrayed frequently as a sellout to the predatory interests of the slaveholders in a game of self-promotion. Fillmore becomes a man who abandoned humane imperatives for a mess of political porridge—a "doughface." Whether or not historical investigation which upsets this conclusion will ever become popularly accepted is of modest import. More revealing is that investigation has revealed the nature of politics in Fillmore's day. Understanding of the unifying force of the political process which he chose eliminates the question of whether his choice was wise or self-serving.

Looking forward from 1850, history supplements the answer. Since his day, not only has every successful movement in American politics required the application of the precept Fillmore learned as a youth in New York politics, but the method of how that precept should be used—coalesce units from the North and the South—has proved to be the touchstone of achievement.

Could Fillmore Have Saved the Union?

Charles M. Snyder

THE *New York Times* of August 23, 1972, contained a column by Vice-president Agnew on the quality of his predecessors in this high office. He singled out Theodore Roosevelt and Harry Truman for honorable mention, but ignored Millard Fillmore. Had he probed more deeply, however, he might have linked the nearly forgotten 13th President to the current theme of his party: the blessings enjoyed by Americans, and the tragedy of polarization by sections, ethnic origins, or income. On the other hand, had Fillmore measured up to Agnew's standards, his nomination would scarcely have served the latter's defense of the prevailing method of selecting Vice-presidents by the presidential nominees, in that Fillmore was nominated by the national convention of his party, in open session, and in competition with other aspirants.

As I have reviewed what I believe to be the thesis of Professor Rayback's writings on President Fillmore I find much to agree with: Fillmore's nationalism; his faith in the democratic process; his thorough grounding in politics; his "unshakable faith in the beneficence of trade and commerce"; his statesmanship; his courage; his flexibility; and his coolness under pressure.[1] Where I differ, it is largely a matter of emphasis, a question of adjectives, and impressions gathered from newly discovered Fillmore papers.[2]

In his biography Rayback objects to dismissing Fillmore with the stereotype, "a vain and handsome mediocrity." I agree. I would prefer self-confident to vain. And as for handsome, I suppose it is a matter of personal preference. But we would have to accept the fact that Fillmore's generation thought him strikingly handsome. Woman's suffrage would have been a boon to him at the polls and television and motion pictures would have been additional assets.

How often does one, even a past President, receive an unsolicited letter such as this? The writer: a 40-year-old widow of New England antecedents, and editor of a newspaper in Yazoo City, Mississippi. During her brief stopover at Buffalo on a trip to Boston, Fillmore, then 57 and a widower, escorted her to Niagara Falls. It was their only meeting. Returning to her home she regretted that she had failed to see him again.

> There is but one thing I regret, and that is my visit to Buffalo. As I shall never refer to it again . . . I must in justice to myself, beg you, if you ever think of it, to remember that to me there is but one Mr. Fillmore in the world, and but two places: the one where he *is*, and the other where he is *not*.[3]

It is more difficult to evaluate Fillmore's alleged mediocrity, or the charge that he sold out to the predatory interests of slaveholders. But let us defer judgment.

"What was disparagingly reported as Fillmore's overweening personal ambition," Rayback notes, "upon investigation turned into self-sacrifice; his fatal vanity, moreover, became simple dignity." I would suggest, however, that if Fillmore's political ambition was not overweening, it was a powerful spur to his career. Let us glance at the record. Three successful bids for election to the New York State Assembly, four terms in the United States House of Representatives, an unsuccessful race for governor of New York in 1844 as the Whig standard-bearer, a term as comptroller of New York, the first to be elected to this office, an unsuccessful seeker of the vice-presidency in 1844, and a successful candidate in 1848—how can such intensive political activity be written off as self-sacrifice or the behavior of an "almost modest man"?

But he did not stop here. In 1852 he was hopeful of obtaining his party's nomination for a full term; and he came close to getting it. Only after 53 ballots did General Scott's supporters wrest the nomination from him; and four years later he succumbed to presidential nominations by the American and Whig Parties (or what was left of the latter). He finally turned down overtures in 1860 that he make himself available for the presidential nomination of the Constitutional Union Party. Politics was truly his life, and after the glitter of the presidency, he chose not to return to the routine of a law practice despite his former eminence in that profession.

To continue Professor Rayback's evaluation: "He was not a clever politician or an inspiring orator." I find no quarrel here. He was no match for Thurlow Weed in the game of politics. Only as Vice-president and President, when his partisans importuned him to stir himself over the patronage and he found himself thwarted by the pipeline between Weed and the Taylor administration, did he take the offensive. It proved ineffectual. In his own backyard, in Buffalo, Taylor named a blatant Fillmore baiter as collector of the port. Mortified—for the news quickly spread across the state—Fillmore asked for a reconsideration and dispatched Nathan K. Hall, a former congressman and erstwhile law partner, to Washington to intercede with Taylor and Secretary Meredith. Obtaining no satisfaction, Fillmore belatedly hastened to the capital, only to find Taylor immovable. Taylor noted that Allen was recommended by the local congressman, by the Buffalo city council, and by shipowners and shippers along the Great Lakes, and he reminded Fillmore that he had not indicated that Allen was repulsive to him personally, and insisted that he had not intended to embarrass him.

Meanwhile, Weed partisans were boasting, "We could put up a cow against a Fillmore nominee and defeat him."

Later during Fillmore's presidency, the New York State Whig convention of October 1850, presaging the Silver Grey controversy, was a dramatic demonstration of his political failure in his own state. Fillmore's floor leaders insisted upon an unqualified endorsement of the Compromise. They not only failed to get it, but suffered an ignominious defeat when Weed's spokesmen obtained the adoption of a resolution extolling Seward's cogent leadership in the Senate—a blanket approbation of his justification of free-soil on a "higher law" than the Constitution. Without Fillmore's restraining hand to halt them, his disconcerted followers stalked from the hall, demonstrating Weed's mastery and widening the chasm between the Conscience Whigs and Silver Greys.

Two years later Weed and Seward blasted Fillmore's hopes for another term when they fostered Scott's candidacy and almost completely shut him out of the support of his state. Delegates to the nominating convention from western New York, including the member from Buffalo, cast their votes for Scott, leaving only seven "Cotton" Whigs from New York City in the Fillmore ranks. Fourteen additional New York votes would have given him the nomination. No, Fillmore was not suited to joust with Weed; but who was?

Nor was Fillmore a match for Seward on the platform. He had neither his eloquence nor his flair for the dramatic. He was no showman. Yet his simple dignity, his warm smile, his reassuring manner, and his plain and artless delivery were persuasive. In fact, the natural charm of his smile can be likened only to that of President Eisenhower. It scarcely needs to be emphasized that Weed and Seward were immune to this charisma.

His presence on a platform in Buffalo somehow upgraded it and added significance to the occasion. Only once have I found an exception; and this may not have been so much the reaction of his audience as the ensuing response of the press. On the anniversary of Washington's birthday in 1864, in the depth of the Civil War, he addressed a Christian Commission fair in Buffalo. And, in what may have been a departure from his text, he lashed out against the war's cost in lives, freedom, and property.

Three years of war have desolated the fairest portion of our land, loaded the country with debt that the sweat of millions yet unborn must be taxed to pay; arrayed brother against brother, and father against son in mortal combat; deluged our country with fraternal blood; whitened our battlefields with bones of the slain, and darkened the sky with the pall of mourning.[4]

The speech drew the wrath of the press wherever it was reported, and "Copperhead" was not the most derogatory of the epithets.

But, a year later, when the martyred Lincoln's body approached Buffalo, it was Fillmore who was delegated to head a citizens' committee to meet the train and accompany it to the city.

Fillmore's contribution to a broadening role in international relations, particularly in the Far East and Latin America, is obviously significant, and Professor Rayback has made a solid case for it. He saw the need for coal and coaling stations in the Pacific as the American merchant marine turned from sails to steam. Perry's "opening" of Japan reflected this vision. And with the nation's larger cities facing the East Coast, he gave a high priority to rail and canal construction in Central America to link them to California and the Orient. Yet he refused to countenance "gun barrel diplomacy," and rebuked filibusterers seeking to raise the American flag in Nicaragua and Cuba.

In his Hulsemann letter (drafted by Webster) Fillmore expressed the country's sympathy for the oppressed minorities of Europe, who were struggling for home rule and national independence.

On the home front Fillmore took a personal interest in the beautification of Washington. The splendor of the city at the close of the nineteenth century could scarcely have been imagined at mid-century. As Henry Adams noted, "The same rude colony was camped in the same forest with the same unfinished Greek temples for workshops, and sloughs for roads," as it had been in his grandfather's time. In substantially enlarging the capitol in 1851 by the addition of two substantial wings (later to house the Senate and House of Representatives) and a massive dome, Congress turned over many of the details to the Chief Executive. Fillmore worked item by item with architect Thomas Ustick Walter and advised Andrew Jackson Downing on the landscaping of the grounds. He also selected books for a library in the White House, a project initiated by Abigail Fillmore, and, in association with Dorothea Dix, helped design the United States Asylum for Soldiers and Sailors. The public has mistakenly credited him with installing the first bath in the White House. Though a fabrication of a later generation, it remains the best-remembered personal incident relating to Fillmore's presidency.

As an administrator, Fillmore established guidelines for department heads, leaving sufficient latitude for them to operate effectively. And, while the resignation of the Cabinet within hours of Taylor's death had momentarily unnerved him, it permitted him to mold a team in which he had confidence. Subsequent relations were characterized by mutual respect, and even the awesome Webster did not forget that he was the Secretary and not the Chief. In fact, Webster's poor health and long absences from Washington left a good share of his work to the President and subordinates in the department. Fillmore's tenure of office was not tarnished by corruption.

As hosts of the White House the Fillmores opened the mansion to the public with a cordiality unexcelled by their predecessors. A highlight of one of the morning receptions in the winter of 1852 was the presence of Fillmore's aged father. The press noted that it was the first time a President had entertained his father in the White House, and Washington's officialdom and citizens turned out in unprecedented numbers. The resemblance of father and son was unmistakable. Tall, straight, and rawboned, the stereotype of a frontiersman, despite his 80 years, the elder Fillmore was the focus of attention. When a guest inquired of him how he might raise his son to be President, he opined, "Cradle him in a sap trough."

During the last months of Fillmore's tenure visitors frequently filled the saloons and halls to overflowing. The sometimes friendly *Washington Intelligencer* referred to such a reception as

one of the largest and most brilliant ever known here . . . testifying with distinctness the unfeigned respect and regard entertained by the people of our city, residents and strangers, for the excellent Chief Magistrate, whose term of office, equally advantageous to his country and honorable to himself, is so near its close.

But his presidency must stand or fall on the Compromise of 1850. And again, I recommend Rayback's concise analysis of the crisis and the formulation of the so-called compromise. If I have an objection to his explanation, it is that it seems a bit too neat. Did not much of the impetus for free-soilism among Whigs as well as Democrats stem from the urgent appeals of Northern ministers of the gospel expounded from their pulpits, from the literati, such as Lowell and Whittier, and from the presses of free-soil editors? Was this not more consequential than the planning of politicians? Did not Weed gamble upon free-soilism to stay alive politically in New York? Did Seward ingratiate himself with Taylor's advisers to reorient the Whig Party or to collect the patronage of New York State?

Albert D. Kirwin, a noted authority on the crisis, has written that Taylor had led the country to the brink of disaster, and had he lived out his term, the nation might have been torn by disunion and civil war a decade before Lincoln's election.[5] Whether you agree with Kirwin's judgment or not, it is surely an oversimplification to dismiss the Compromise of 1850 as a brief respite in the sectional struggle and a short delay in the coming of the Civil War, leaving the broader issue unresolved. To me, it is more realistic to weigh the crisis in its 1850 dimensions—as Fillmore was called upon to face it.

And for him there was but one answer. Entering manhood 50 years after the birth of the Republic, when Revolutionary War veterans were a part of any Fourth of July audience, the concept of a temporary or transitory Union was almost inconceivable. He had early discarded the provincialism of his frontier childhood and, as a young congressman, had found friends among nationalists from all sections. In piecing together the tariff of 1842, he harmonized the special interests of a diversifying society. And now confronting a sectional impasse he sought a solution through compromise. Obviously, he was providing the Weed-Seward faction with an issue which could destroy him. But he let it be known that he would accept the compromise, whether it was adopted as a single omnibus or as separate bills, and he capped it with his signature upon the controversial Fugitive Slave bill.

Overlooked as historians have turned to the turmoil attending the Kansas-Nebraska bill is the fact that Fillmore ended his tenure of office amidst the plaudits of a grateful nation. The six-year roadblock was removed, and the ominous Nashville Convention disbanded. California's gold was intoxicating the economy; demonstrations against the Fugitive Slave Act were fewer now and receiving less attention than before. People were more relaxed than at any moment since Texas statehood. It appeared to many Americans on March 4, 1853, that reason had triumphed over passion, and nationalism over sectionalism. And countless Americans attributed a good share of their blessings to Millard Fillmore.

Having already gone down a lonely road, permit me to take one more step. Suppose the egotistical Webster had seen himself as others saw him at this moment and been realistic enough to transfer a handful of his votes in the nominating convention to Fillmore and make possible his nomination. Would it have made any difference?

Possibly not. Seemingly, the Democrats would have won in any event by endorsing the Compromise of 1850 and using it to unify their party; though Fillmore would have been a more formidable candidate than Scott. But, suppose he had won. Is it possible that he would have repudiated the Compromise and fallen into the Kansas-Nebraska morass? Hardly.

Holman Hamilton has argued that even at this late hour under competent leadership land grants to railroads and colleges and homesteads to farmers might have girded the Union.[6] But obviously, Pierce and Buchanan did not provide such leadership. What about Fillmore?

Chester Alan Arthur:
"Better Than Anyone Expected"

Thomas C. Reeves

ON THE morning of July 2, 1881, a small, shabbily dressed man was captured by a policeman as he raced toward an exit at the Baltimore and Potomac railroad station in Washington, D.C. Seconds earlier he had fired two bullets into President James A. Garfield. "I must arrest you," the excited policeman gasped. "All right," came the quiet reply. "I did it and will go to jail for it. I am a Stalwart, and Arthur will be President."[1]

In the eyes of many Americans Vice-president Chester A. Arthur represented much of what was wrong with contemporary politics. He was the boss, the spoilsman, the election fixer who perverted the democratic process for his own profit. E. L. Godkin, editor of *The Nation,* outlined his political career and concluded, "It is out of this mess of filth that Mr. Arthur will go to the Presidential chair in case of the President's death."[2] The *New York Times* commented, "While his succession to the Presidency of the United States depends simply on the issue of a strong man's struggle with death, Gen. Arthur is about the last man who would be considered eligible to that position, did the choice depend on the voice either of a majority of his own party or of a majority of the people of the United States."[3] The assassin, Charles Guiteau, claimed to be on intimate terms with Arthur, and more than a few angry citizens in those hot summer days 93 years ago were willing to believe that he had been the agent of a power-hungry and ruthless Vice-president.

During the more than two months in which Garfield clung to

59

life the public learned much about the man who was his constitutional successor. Arthur had been born in Fairfield, Vermont,
in 1829, the first son and fifth child of a highly literate and pious
Baptist preacher and his wife.[4] In 1835 the family moved to
New York State where Chester spent most of the rest of his life.
He was graduated from Union College in 1848, taught school
briefly, and traveled to New York City to earn admission to the
bar. As an attorney he won some local attention by participating
in the Lemmon case, which freed slaves traveling through the
free state, and by successfully representing Elizabeth Jennings,
a Negro schoolteacher who sued after being routed from a segre-
gated New York City streetcar. Arthur became seriously interested in politics in 1854 and attended a meeting of free-soilers
that was instrumental in creating a Republican Party in New
York. He was greatly influenced by Thurlow Weed, and with his
help won appointment to the staff of Governor Edwin D. Morgan, a powerful figure in the Whig and Republican Parties.

When the Civil War broke out Morgan appointed Arthur engi-
neer-in-chief of the New York militia. The young man's unusual
executive ability and devotion to hard work earned him promotions to the rank of quartermaster general. When Morgan and his
staff left office and lost their commissions on the first day of 1863
Arthur failed to reenlist, in large part out of respect for the sympathies of his Virginia-born wife, Ellen, whom he married in
1859. For the remainder of the conflict he practiced law, spe-
cializing in the handling of war claims.

One of Arthur's clients, a wealthy and unscrupulous New York
hatter named Tom Murphy, became a close friend. Together, as
members of the conservative wing of New York's G.O.P., dominated by Weed, Morgan, and William Henry Seward, they
worked on campaigns and collected political assessments with
an eye toward obtaining political office. By 1867 Arthur sat on
the executive committee of New York City's Republican Central
Committee; a year later he chaired the State Committee's top
committee and was a leader in the drive to elect Grant. At some
point in 1869 Murphy made an arrangement with William Marcy
Tweed, an acquaintance of more than a decade, that landed Ar-

CHESTER ALAN ARTHUR
October 5, 1830–November 18, 1886
The Twenty-first President of The United States

thur the office of counsel to the New York City Tax Commission, a post that paid $10,000 a year. Before long he won the admiration of New York's new Senator, arrogant and elegant Roscoe Conkling.

In July 1870, Grant nominated Tom Murphy to be Collector of the Port of New York. With Conkling's help, the controversial nomination cleared the Senate. At that point New York Republicanism was securely in the hands of a faction led by Conkling and containing Murphy and Arthur, a faction possessing the full confidence of the President. Murphy carried out a purge of political opponents in the Customhouse and was forced to resign in late 1871 amid charges of corruption. In his place, at Murphy's urging, Grant selected Arthur.

The New York Customhouse was the largest single federal office in the nation, collecting about 75 percent of the country's customs receipts. It was also the greatest single source of patronage. While ideally the Collector should have possessed considerable commercial and administrative experience, in fact he was usually a politician in charge of dispensing spoils and levying campaign assessments on employee paychecks. Collector Arthur was popular with both businessmen and politicians. He was tactful, sophisticated, dapper, and suave—a gentleman whose appearance, manners, education, and membership in the elite Union League Club marked him as a large cut above the political hacks with whom he frequently associated. His knowledge of law and commercial transactions, as well as his Whiggish, wholly orthodox views on fiscal conservatism, the tariff, and limited government were welcomed by merchants and bankers. At the same time, Arthur's views on the spoils system, in spite of pious statements to the contrary, were clearly those of his predecessors, fellow collectors, and political associates. His experienced special deputy surveyor would call him "probably the ablest politician that has ever filled the collector's chair." Veteran Republican leader Chauncey Depew would describe him as "one of the most rigid of organization and machine men in his days of local leadership."[5] Arthur resisted moves by civil service reformers to have appointments and promotions tied to competitive examinations; he complied with requests for patronage emanating from all levels within the G.O.P. whenever possible; he bitterly opposed efforts to reduce salaries and personnel in the Customhouse; and he was actively involved in the assessment of officeholders, producing sizable sums of money for campaigns. Arthur dominated the influential New York City Republican machine. He and many colleagues appeared annually at New York State Republican conventions to manipulate proceedings to the Conkling faction's advantage. In 1876 he led a contingent of officeholders to the national convention and campaigned openly for Conkling's nomination as President.

Arthur was the first Collector in a quarter century to serve a full four years. His survival and his reappointment in 1875 were due not only to his dexterous and at times clever management of a difficult job but even more to the power of the Grant-Conkling alliance.

The new occupant of the White House in 1877, Rutherford B. Hayes, assumed office holding a grudge against Conkling for his tepid support during the campaign. At the same time he was sincerely attracted by the civil service reform movement, an increasingly popular drive to take politics out of government employment. To initiate reform and also to transfer Conkling's authority in New York to more sympathetic Republicans, Hayes launched a penetrating investigation into the source of much of the Senator's power, the nation's largest customhouse. A blue-ribbon panel, after several months of study, documented waste, inefficiency, political favoritism, and widespread corruption in the place of business, and Arthur and two of his lieutenants were publicly requested to resign. Arthur refused to step down, forcing the President to remove him from office. After a further Customhouse inquiry and a fierce battle between Conkling and the administration, the ex-Collector returned to his law practice.

In 1879 Chester Arthur was president of the Republican Central Committee, the ruling body of city Republicanism, and chairman of the party's state committee. He worked diligently to strengthen his faction's position and constructed an impressive record as a political boss. In the elections of that year Republi-

cans won every state office but that of State Engineer, and solidly controlled the legislature. Foremost in the minds of Conkling and Arthur was the effort to win a third term for General
Grant in 1880, a victory that would overcome the defeat at the
hands of Hayes. Pro-Grant spoilsmen in Pennsylvania and Illinois, as well as New York, looked to the stolid little general for
the reinvigoration of their political machines. The "Stalwarts," as
they became known, carefully planned Grant's moves for more
than two years, in anticipation of the national convention in Chicago.

Arthur arrived in the Windy City five days ahead of the convention's scheduled opening to muster support for his candidate.
He sat next to Conkling at the head of New York's large delegation and participated in every Stalwart move to nominate Grant.
He was one of 306 delegates who stood fast for the general until
the convention settled for a compromise candidate, James A.
Garfield of Ohio.

It seemed logical that a Stalwart would be chosen to comple-
ment the ticket as a gesture toward party unity. And New York
was pivotal in a national election. A former governor of Ohio,
without authorization from his state delegation, approached
Conkling minutes after Garfield's selection and offered him the
right to name a vice-presidential candidate. Conkling said he
would leave the matter to his state caucus, and issued a call to
delegates. Two of Arthur's friends overheard the conversation
and, after winning Arthur's assent, scurried through hotel corri-
dors to inform allies of the impending meeting. Garfield sought
New Yorker Levi P. Morton as his running mate, and had sent
the chairman of the Ohio delegation to tender the offer. But
Morton was discouraged by a friend from accepting the bid, and
when the caucus met he withdrew his name. Only 42 of the 70
New York delegates attended the caucus, and most of them
were New York City Stalwarts. On a voice vote Chester Arthur
was chosen to be the nominee. Conkling was opposed to Arthur's
decision to run, but his anger subsided shortly after the convention placed his lieutenant on the national ticket. The former
Ohio governor who had offered Conkling the nomination pri-

vately sent his apologies to Hayes, assuring the President that Arthur had not crossed his mind when he spoke with the New York Senator. Young Henry Cabot Lodge soon wrote, "No one will abandon Garfield on account of Arthur," and the ticket would benefit from the "direction of the shrewdest political manager in the country."⁶ Godkin wryly considered another side of the nomination: ". . . there is no place in which his powers of mischief will be so small as in the Vice Presidency, and it will remove him during a great part of the year from his own field of activity." The editor continued, "It is true General Garfield, if elected, may die during his term of office, but this is too unlikely a contingency to be worth making extraordinary provision for."⁷

Arthur did not leave New York during the campaign, but he contributed significantly to the Republican victory. He coordinated scores of rallies and meetings, acquired the services of speechmakers, supervised the creation and distribution of assessment circulars, raised large sums of money from businessmen, and took personal charge of the travels of Conkling and Grant through the Midwest. The Garfield-Arthur ticket came out ahead in November with a nationwide margin of 7,018 votes; the count in the Electoral College was 214 to 155. New York was carried by the G.O.P. A decrease in Democratic strength in New York City was the deciding factor. If the state's 35 electoral votes had gone to the opposition, Winfield Scott Hancock, rather than Garfield, would have been President. The editor of the *New York Times* wrote that Arthur's services were "of the highest importance to the Republican Party" and that his management of the campaign in New York was distinguished by "ability and quiet strength."⁸

Even before his inauguration, Garfield fell under the influence of James G. Blaine, a clever and ambitious politician and one of Conkling's archenemies. New York Stalwarts fared poorly in the selection of Garfield's Cabinet, and open warfare soon erupted between Conklingites and the administration. In late March 1881, Garfield appointed a Blaine supporter Collector of the New York Customhouse, an attempt to smash Conkling's remaining authority and win firm control of the G.O.P. in New York. Arthur sided with his longtime colleagues throughout the struggle. He lobbied

in Albany during a Senate race against an administration candidate. He signed a petition condemning Garfield's choice for
Collector. He hosted an anti-administration strategy session at
his home. And when Conkling and Thomas Platt dramatically re-
signed from the Senate to protest confirmation of the new Collector, the Vice-president traveled to Albany to campaign for their
reelection. For weeks he cajoled and browbeat weary Republicans in the hope they would defy their party standard-bearer.

Arthur suffered blistering criticism in the press for his opposition to the President. The *Chicago Evening Journal* found his activities "reprehensible and disgusting in the second officer of the
Government."[9] Thomas Nast published a scathing cartoon por-
traying Arthur as a bootblack for Conkling and Platt; under it
was the caption, "I did not engage you, Vice-President Arthur,
to do this kind of work."[10]

When Garfield was shot, as he walked arm in arm with Blaine
through the Washington railway depot, Arthur was returning
home from Albany following a week's labor on behalf of his Stalwart friends. News of Guiteau's boast spread as rapidly as the
story that Garfield was already dead. The Vice-president stepped
off of a steamer in the late morning of July 2 to discover himself
one of the most despised political figures in American history.

Despite his reputation as a hardboiled, cynical spoilsman, Arthur was an emotional and sensitive man who suffered keenly
when assailed by critics. The sudden turn of events left him overcome with grief; friends likened his condition to the breakdown
he had suffered a year and a half earlier at the death of his wife.
In public, however, Arthur was a model of dignity. His sober
public statements won immediate admiration. He disassociated
himself from the losing struggle of the Stalwarts in Albany. He
spurned the suggestion that he assume office before Garfield's
death. Newspapers and journals tempered their hostility somewhat; Arthur was described as a gentleman, and his conduct during the crisis was considered unexceptionable. There were even
those who contended that Arthur would change dramatically
once he found himself in the White House. Governor Foster of
Ohio predicted, "The people and the politicians will find that

Vice-president Arthur and President Arthur are different men."[11] As weeks passed a mood of hopefulness tinged with optimism seemed to emerge from the rage of the first weeks of July.

Garfield died during the evening of September 19, 1881, and in the pre-dawn hours of the next day Arthur took the oath of office in his New York home. He was the nation's 21st President. "No man ever assumed the Presidency under more trying circumstances," the *New York Times* commented, "no President has needed more the generous appreciation, the indulgent forbearance of his fellow-citizens. . . . He is a much better and broader man than the majority of those with whom his recent political career has been identified."[12]

The obstacles standing between Chester Arthur and a successful presidency were enormous. His political experience had been restricted almost exclusively to one state, and his knowledge of national and international affairs was limited to what any reasonably curious New Yorker might cull from the local press. Unlike his three predecessors who succeeded to the presidency—John Tyler, Millard Fillmore, and Andrew Johnson—Arthur did not bring a positive national reputation to the White House. Moreover, the G.O.P. was seriously divided, threatening stiff opposition no matter what the future course of action. Republican congressmen were not likely to unite behind the new President. All members of Garfield's Cabinet were thought certain to resign. And Blaine, John Sherman, and perhaps a dozen other Republican leaders were soon expected to begin jockeying for the 1884 nomination. None of the other Vice-presidents catapulted into the White House had been chosen to succeed themselves. And Hayes' weak performance had illustrated the handicaps imposed upon a Chief Executive by the likelihood of a single term.

On the other hand, Arthur was intelligent, had extensive administrative experience, and enjoyed a number of battleworn friends, such as former Governor Morgan, who might give useful counsel. Of late he had earned much public sympathy; a moratorium was in effect on critical inquiries into his past, and most Americans were eager for his success. Then, too, the role of his office at the time was such that it was perhaps within Arthur's reach, despite the obstacles, to win the trust and affection of his countrymen. The theory of the presidency from Grant to McKinley was based firmly on Whig doctrine; the Chief Executive was responsible largely for the execution rather than the initiation of legislation. The impeachment of Johnson and the weakness of Grant had shifted a great deal of power from the executive to the legislative branch, and the Capitol rather than the White House was the hub of action in Washington. The close division of party strength prohibited Presidents from commanding majorities in both houses long enough to push through legislation had they so desired. Party organizations lacked coherence and were unable to discipline legislators. Many contemporaries were convinced that the Senate dominated the government. Senator George F. Hoar wrote that each of his colleagues "kept his own orbit and shone in his own sphere, within which he tolerated no intrusion from the President or from anybody else."[13] Hayes and Garfield restored some of the influence of their office by challenging Conkling, but they rarely exercised initiative in legislative matters. To be an acceptable and perhaps even popular President, Arthur was required to be a dignified representative of the American people, as well as an honest and reasonably efficient administrator. He would have to walk fairly close to his predecessor's footsteps. And he would find it profitable to be prudent in the use of executive authority. An admirer advised, "What the nation needs most at present, is rest. We all are worn out with watching—& when people are very tired, they are apt to be irritable, unreasonable & ready to quarrel on small provocation. If a doctor could lay his finger on the public pulse, his prescription would be, perfect quiet."[14]

Arthur made several attempts to retain members of Garfield's Cabinet in his administration; except in the case of Robert Lincoln, he was unsuccessful. The new Cabinet was composed, by and large, of enlightened Stalwarts. The President's selections met with general approval. Few complaints arose from the hundreds of appointments made throughout the country. The anticipated political purge failed to materialize. In fact, New York Conklingites complained bitterly about their former leader's unwillingness to reward them with public office.

Arthur's messages to Congress contained scores of solid suggestions and recommendations; one historian has called them "remarkable documents" that "should make one wonder whether or not history's verdict regarding Arthur is correct."[15] But, for the most part, they fell on deaf ears. Congress was without strong leadership, and its members seemed interested mainly in local affairs. The great self-satisfaction of the 1880s, which seems so curious in retrospect, demanded little of Senators and Representatives.

The President's handling of the major legislative issues he faced won widespread applause. He vetoed a bill restricting Chinese immigration but signed a similar measure when it contained a revision thought to be more acceptable to the Chinese government. Public opinion was solidly in favor of such restrictions, and Arthur made it clear in his veto message that he accepted the view of the majority. On August 1, 1882, he vetoed a notorious River and Harbor bill, a move favored by leaders of the press and the business community. He became a vocal supporter of civil service reform and signed the famous Pendleton Act of 1883. His "conversion" to the policy, after a quarter-century of spoils politics, occurred when Republicans were dealt crushing defeats at the polls in 1882 and when it became obvious that identification with the spoils system was a political liability. Still, Arthur's support was appreciated and considered enlightened at the time.

In foreign affairs, the administration was only mildly active. It left no monuments to diplomatic achievement but at the President's urging, important steps were taken to inaugurate a new Navy.

The Chief Executive attracted much attention as an elegant and fastidious host. Under his direction the Executive Mansion was handsomely redecorated, and he initiated a series of personal and public entertainments that elevated White House social life to a peak it would rarely, if ever, reach again. In less than a full term the President gave some fifty state dinners and enjoyed innumerable private suppers with large and small groups of friends. At one formal dinner 21 courses were served. At a musical entertainment featuring Madame Christine Nilsson, covers were laid for 54, and there were 378 glasses on the table to accommodate the varieties of wine. After one such occasion, Mrs. Blaine wrote to her daughter, "The dinner was extremely elegant, hardly a trace of the old White House taint being perceptible anywhere, the flowers, the damask, the silver, the attendants, all showing the latest style and an abandon in expense and taste."[16] Rutherford B. Hayes read reports of these pleasures and snarled, "Nothing like it ever before in the Executive Mansion—liquor, snobbery, and worse."[17]

Arthur's personal appearance prompted as much comment as his social accomplishments, for not since Franklin Pierce had Washington seen a President so devoted to his attire. His clothes were made by a well-known New York tailor whose high prices reflected the status of his customers. The President spent considerable time as well as money on his apparel; one day, it was said, he tried on 20 pairs of trousers made to his measurements before selecting one to his taste. Thomas Platt later called him "the beau-ideal of the American citizen."

Six feet two in height, symmetrically built; a head adorned with silken, wavy hair, always carefully combed; whiskers of the Burnside variety, invariably trimmed to the perfection point; blue, kindly eyes, straight nose, ruddy cheeks—these and his polished manners gave him the address of a veritable Chesterfield.[18]

The President's handsome carriage, complete with monogrammed lap robes and expensively outfitted coachmen, was a familiar sight in the nation's capital. While walking or riding the streets of Washington, Arthur seemed pleased by salutations and invariably acknowledged them by lifting his hat and making an elaborate bow, without regard to the social position of the citizen involved. At his death a local newspaper would declare, "No president since the war has been so universally popular here."[19]

But beneath the gay facade and far from the public eye was a man described by a cousin as "sick in body and soul."[20] Arthur had never coveted the presidency, and he found its duties and responsibilities extremely distasteful. His social activities and frequent trips were channels of escape from an office that rewarded him with little more than worry and fatigue. A man well placed in the administration thought him "in a measure stunned, uncertain, and in any event moody, possibly unhappy."[21] Again, his cousin noted in his diary, "Chester says with Solomon 'All is vanity & vexation of spirit; and His golden chain is but a chain at last.' "[22]

But the cares of office were only one of the wellsprings of Arthur's deep unhappiness. He had never overcome his grief caused by the death of his wife. Moreover, he was physically ill to a degree unknown by all but a few intimates. Partly this was due to a longtime habit of staying up until the early hours of every morning dining, drinking, and smoking cigars with close friends. His weight soared to almost 250 pounds at a time when his exercise was limited to a few walks every week and some brief horseback riding. Far more serious was the fact that Arthur became afflicted with Bright's disease, a kidney ailment thought certain to be fatal. Physicians apparently diagnosed the problem in the summer of 1882, within the first year of Arthur's presidency. During the remainder of his term in office various observers described the President as being in poor health, but only one or two of his closest friends were permitted to know the seriousness of his discomfort. While on a trip to Florida in April 1883, Arthur almost succumbed to a sudden illness. In great pain, he privately told the attending physician of his kidney ailment. The secret was kept until 1911.[23]

During 1884 Arthur began to debilitate noticeably. He knew well that he could never live out a second term and did little to seek the presidential nomination. Those who were not privy to Arthur's secret exerted some effort on his behalf and were puzzled and upset by his uncharacteristic unwillingness to enter a political fight with gusto. One young partisan, the postmaster of Washington, D.C., and a delegate to the national convention, was privately asked by the President to refrain from campaigning on his behalf and to ask his friends to do the same. He dismissed the request as modesty and traveled to Chicago an avid Arthur man.

After the convention Arthur told his friend of his illness and confided to him that he envisioned only a few months or at most a
couple of years of life. He explained that he had refrained from
taking himself out of the race officially because the nation would
have concluded that he feared defeat at the convention or at the
polls. The postmaster waited until 1933 to relate these events to a
historian.[24]

By 1884 there were grounds for believing that Arthur would be
denied the presidential nomination regardless of his personal efforts and despite the admiration he enjoyed in many quarters. Republicans sustained severe losses in the congressional elections of
1882, and in New York the G.O.P. suffered what was then, in the
words of Robert Marcus, "the greatest state election defeat in
American history."[25] Most Republicans blamed the President for
the damage done in his home state. Secretary of the Treasury
Charles Folger won the gubernatorial nomination over the popular Republican incumbent, it was widely thought, through
trickery employed by a few of Arthur's longtime associates. In
fact, Arthur himself played no role in helping Folger win the
nomination and was severely criticized by Stalwarts for failing
to lend support to his Cabinet member's campaign. Nevertheless, the overwhelming triumph by Grover Cleveland and other
state Democrats was attributed to the White House. Stalwart
losses in Pennsylvania and in Ohio the following year were
heralded as signs that voters were no longer interested in men
who had supported Grant.

From mid-1883 newspaper polls showed consistently that
Blaine was favored over Arthur and that the President could not
win in all-important New York if nominated. The influential reform wing of the Republican Party supported neither man.
Clearly, the badly fractured G.O.P. could not be expected to
unify around the incumbent.

Furthermore, the administration failed to secure convictions of
leaders in the Star Route frauds, one of the more grandiose swin-
dles of the era. One leader, Stephen Dorsey, had been a close
friend and political associate of Arthur's, and critics contended
that the President had not prosecuted him with sufficient vigor.

A mild recession had also loomed across the nation in 1882, causing dissatisfaction. Efforts to lower the tariff were stymied in Congress, and again the administration shouldered blame.

Blaine won the nomination easily, reformers bolted the ticket, and Cleveland narrowly won the presidential contest. Arthur retired to his home in New York, became increasingly ill, and died in November 1886. The day before he suffered a fatal cerebral hemorrhage he ordered the great bulk of his papers burned, and sent his son along with a workman to supervise the destruction. Until very recently he remained our most obscure Chief Executive. But Arthur was surely attempting to obliterate his long and fascinating career as the "Gentleman Boss" rather than conceal his record as President.

Arthur was a better President than anyone expected him to be. Given his background, the circumstances of his elevation, his mandate from the public, his divided party, his lack of presidential authority, and his personal melancholy and deteriorating physical condition, it is somewhat surprising that he fared as well as he did. Contemporary opinion, especially near the end of the administration, was quite complimentary and became even more positive during the next two decades. The evaluation by Alexander McClure is by no means exceptional: "No man ever entered the Presidency so profoundly and widely distrusted as Chester Alan Arthur, and no one ever retired from the highest civil trust of the world more generally respected, alike by friend and foe."[26]

The Arthur administration calmed a nation jolted by assassination. It was virtually free of corruption. It carried out its duties with relative impartiality. It confined its aspirations to boundaries set by public opinion. At that point in our nation's history only a few citizens requested more. The President did not inspire, challenge, or lead in the colorful and dramatic way that would later seem attractive. But such a posture by an "accidental" President in the early 1880s would have brought outcry from Congress, disdain from the likes of Jay Gould and Andrew Carnegie, and more than a little scorn from the American people. William E. Chandler wrote of Arthur: "His conservative administration of the government commanded universal confidence, preserved public order and promoted business activity. If his conduct of affairs be criticized as lacking aggressiveness, it may confidently be replied that aggressiveness would have been unfortunate, if not disastrous. Rarely has there been a time when an indiscreet president could have wrought more mischief. It was not a time for showy exploits of brilliant experimentation. Above all else, the people needed rest from the strain and excitement into which the assassination of their president had plunged them."[27]

When the statue of Arthur was unveiled in Madison Square in 1899 Elihu Root gave the major address. His lengthy eulogy of the 21st President concluded:

The genuineness of his patriotism, the integrity of his purpose and the wisdom of his conduct changed general distrust to universal confidence, re-established popular belief in the adequacy of our constitutional system in all emergencies, and restored an abiding trust in the perpetuity of our Government. He himself greatly aided to make true the memorable words of his first inaugural: "Men may die, but the fabrics of our free institutions remain unshaken." . . . With proud and sensitive reticence he had suffered much from calumny. Its completest refutation was the demonstration of what he was. And he was always the same. The noble form of which all America was proud, as it bore with dignity and flawless honor the Chief Magistracy of the greatest of republics, was none other than the simple and true American gentleman who walked with us among our homes and to whose memory we offer this poor tribute.[28]

The audience applauded warmly. It was still the late nineteenth century.

Chester Alan Arthur Reconsidered

Kenneth E. Davison

Historical anniversaries have a way of reviving interest in events and personalities long forgotten or neglected. Along with the approaching bicentennial of the American Revolution, our national memory is now turning toward what was formerly one of the most ignored and least admired periods of our past, the last third of the nineteenth century. Already a major reconsideration of these years is underway.

The contributors to this volume are scholars noted for their leadership in the political reinterpretation of the Golden Age. I would particularly recognize the contribution of our editor, Harry J. Sievers, S.J., who is the author of a definitive three-volume biography of President Benjamin Harrison, an ambitious project launched in 1949 and successfully completed in 1968.

In preparing my comments on Professor Reeves' paper concerning Chester A. Arthur, I was compelled to change some of my favorite notions about the American presidency, and to acknowledge some evidence which had eluded me for 25 years.

First, more than any other state in the Union, indeed more than any other two states combined, New York has dominated the office of President and Vice-president from the beginning of our constitutional history. This volume is focused upon the six Empire State Presidents—Van Buren, Fillmore, Arthur, Cleveland, and the two Roosevelts. I suppose some claim might also be made for Dwight D. Eisenhower, since he was a resident of New York State when first elected to the White House. But what I did not realize before, is how utterly New York has figured in the history of the vice-presidency of the United States. Alexander Hamilton, a New Yorker, created the office of Vice-president at the Constitutional Convention. Paradoxically, three men whose own careers were inextricably bound up with Hamilton's political fortunes, became the first three occupants of the position Hamilton invented—John Adams, Thomas Jefferson, and that other fascinating figure of early New York politics, Aaron Burr.

Burr became the first of ten New York men to be elected to the second highest office in the land. He was followed by George Clinton, Daniel D. Tompkins, Martin Van Buren, Millard Fillmore, William A. Wheeler, Chester A. Arthur, Levi P. Morton, Theodore Roosevelt, and James Sherman—four Democrats, one Whig, and five Republicans. More important, four of these statesmen ultimately became President of the United States. In this respect New York's record compares very favorably with the other states of the Union. While Massachusetts and Indiana have each provided the nation with four Vice-presidents, only John Adams and Calvin Coolidge, both elected from the Bay State, have become President in their own right.

Second, as an Ohioan, I knew that my state had provided more than its share of Presidents (however distinguished), but I never recognized before the obvious lack of Vice-presidents from the Buckeye State.

Third, the highly successful Republican strategy of constructing a national ticket featuring Ohioans paired with New Yorkers should be observed. Beginning with the Hayes and Wheeler candidacies in 1876, the Republicans used the same winning Ohio-New York formula in three subsequent elections: Garfield and Arthur (1880); McKinley and Roosevelt (1900); and Taft and Sherman (1908).

Chester Alan Arthur, the subject of Professor Reeves' forthcoming full-scale biography, has long been one of the least known of American Chief Executives. The usual textbook account portrays him as a "gentleman boss" and spoilsman who was suddenly catapulted into national prominence, first, by a political bargain between Half-Breeds and Stalwarts which put him on the Republican ticket in June 1880; and second, by becoming

Chief Executive only 16 months later through the tragedy of Garfield's death from the effects of an assassin's bullet.

The nation, we have been taught, shuddered at the terrible prospect of Chester A. Arthur running the country. "My God, Chet Arthur President of the United States!" is a favorite quotation used by many classroom teachers. But Arthur, the customary treatment continues, did a remarkable aboutface, turned his back upon his former associates, and to the surprise of everyone became a rather good President, certainly not the failure he was expected to be. The traditional view of Arthur concludes by sadly noting that his show of independence and honesty cost him the 1884 Republican nomination, and with it the opportunity to be elected in his own right as Theodore Roosevelt managed to do in 1904.

This general concept of President Arthur persisted for a long time, and seemed likely to survive indefinitely, since Arthur deliberately destroyed many of his personal and presidential papers a few days prior to his death in November 1886, thus denying to historians valuable primary sources necessary for an objective evaluation of his presidency. Arthur's place in history, judged at least by the historians and political scientists who participated in three separate polls of 1948, 1955, and 1962 has remained virtually constant. Arthur has been assigned a position in the presidential ranking game near the bottom of the average or middle group; to be exact, his rank has fluctuated from 17 to 20 to 19. One of my beloved mentors, the late Wilfred E. Binkley, a prominent Republican political scientist and Gilded Age scholar who took part in both Schlesinger polls, ranked Arthur as below average, or "D" in a standard grading system. (See Appendix.)

In the summer of 1962 my family and I took a New England vacation, and along the way we visited the Arthur birthplace in Vermont, where we collected the usual tourist pictures and a neatly printed blue brochure which I still own. At the time, it seemed to me that, in pursuing my hobby of American Presidents, I could safely close the file on Chester A. Arthur. In fact, until 1971, I learned very little more about Arthur—just a few personal items of a comparative nature: he was one of three American Presidents whose father was a minister; like four other Presidents he earned Phi Beta Kappa honors in college; he was one of five widowers to occupy the White House; he liked to fish; he was a tall man, exceeded only by Lincoln and Jefferson among our Presidents; he was one of the youngest ex-Presidents to die; he enjoyed rich foods, and his gourmet appetite suggested a possible reason for his early demise.

Out of such scattered facts I formed an opinion of Chester A. Arthur. And I was in good company. Henry Steele Commager, reviewing George Frederick Howe's *Chester A. Arthur: A Quarter Century of Machine Politics* for the *New York Herald Tribune* in 1934, observed: "Professor Howe's book is the first biography of Arthur which has been written; it is likely to be the last. There is on the whole little to say about Arthur; that little Professor Howe has said as well as it could be said. The limitations of the subject are discouraging; the limitations of material intimidating. . . ."[1]

What happens when a dedicated scholar goes to work on such a problem makes for a fascinating historiographical case study. The factual record is substantially corrected, updated, and enlarged. In the process our inherited assumptions about a bygone era receive a sharp jolt. During the past several years Professor Thomas C. Reeves has provided historians with a fresh view of Chester A. Arthur through a series of carefully researched and well-written articles on various aspects of Arthur's life and career.[2] His excellent essays break new ground and upset many older ideas. Arthur's birthplace turns out not to be the real birthplace at all; Arthur's accepted birthdate of October 5, 1830, which is in every standard reference work and textbook, and even on his tombstone, is wrong. He was actually born a year earlier. Even the presumed burial-site of the President is not the precise spot. A recent account linking President Arthur with a "mysterious lady friend"[3] whom the widower President met at least once, at his suggestion, while he was Chief Executive, becomes much less daring and sinister in Professor Reeves' identification of Julia Sand as an invalided dwarf whose avid interest in politics prompted her to write a series of letters to Arthur full of political advice. His visit to her New York City home was hardly an assignation, but simply a presidential courtesy toward an unusual correspondent. Furthermore, this single social call lasted but an hour, and was witnessed by other members of the household who remained in the room during the entire time. Details of Arthur's early life and career are set forth in other articles published by Reeves since 1969. For example, President Arthur's surprise visit to Yellowstone National Park in 1883 receives new emphasis in the perspective of present-day concerns for conservation of our natural resources.

Even more significant is Reeves' discussion of Arthur's health problem, in particular, how it sheds light upon his course as President, and especially, his loss of the 1884 Republican nomination to Blaine. Arthur was informed by his doctors after he became President that he was a dying man. The President's secret was kept from all but a few close friends and political associates. Arthur knew that, even if nominated and elected, he could not live long enough to complete a second term. He therefore discouraged efforts in his behalf, and James G. Blaine became the party's standard-bearer.

These are but a few of the new insights we now have into Arthur's life. They have been made possible by the discovery and recovery of literally thousands of documents relative to it unearthed by the persistent detective work of Reeves, in association with descendants of Arthur and his contemporaries, plus the work of some enterprising librarians and private parties. Happily, Professor Commager's gloomy forecast of a dead end for Arthur scholarship is about to be discarded by the appearance of a new biography written by Thomas C. Reeves, and based upon the newly acquired documents. I, for one, anxiously await the Reeves book. Meantime, I wish to make a few comments from the perspective of some recent research in the papers of one of Arthur's contemporaries, Rutherford B. Hayes.

First, the Republican victory in November 1880 may at least in part be attributed to the success of Hayes in restoring confidence in his party, and in winning respect for himself after a bitterly contested election. Not only did Hayes stoutly defend his legal right to the presidency, he recovered and strengthened the power and prestige of the executive branch after it had reached a low ebb under Grant. By naming his own Cabinet, by resisting legislative riders to appropriation bills, by challenging the hegemony of the Senate, and by elevating the tone of official life, President Hayes restored confidence in presidential leadership and redressed the balance of power among the three branches of government. Unable to function as a legislative leader without a working majority, he resorted to administrative action to win respect for his office.

Second, the social side of the Hayes administration is not well enough known. Professor Reeves speaks of Arthur's entertainment policy and sharply contrasts it with the Hayes era. In fact, Mrs. Hayes was the first of "the new women" in the White House, and the Hayeses set a very high standard for frequent and expensive entertainment.[4] The often-mentioned sobriquet of "Lemonade Lucy" and the overemphasis on the lack of wine at White House dinners during her era distorts the situation. She never belonged to the Women's Christian Temperance Union, and it was President Hayes, not the First Lady, who instituted the temperance regime, and this he did for the political advantage it would give to Republicans in the extremely close elections of his time. Hayes was not a teetotaler—he frequently ordered whiskey for his troops in the Civil War, and his home at Fremont, Ohio, had an excellent wine cellar.

Mrs. James G. Blaine is a source of unflattering observations on the Hayeses' social policy, and her animus to Lucy Hayes is well documented.[5] Mrs. Blaine was virtually never in the White House socially or officially in the Hayes period. She also missed a good chance of becoming First Lady herself when Hayes narrowly defeated her husband for the party's presidential nomination on the seventh ballot of the 1876 Republican National Convention.

Hamilton J. Eckenrode's undocumented 1930 biography of Hayes is not reliable on factual details, and should be used with great care. Eckenrode did not spend any time examining the

Hayes Papers at Speigel Grove (Hayes' Fremont, Ohio, home and site of the R. B. Hayes Presidential Library), and his research assistant spent less than a fortnight working with the manuscript collection, which at that time was far less organized, and not at all item-indexed as it is today.

Arthur surely was a more fastidious President in his dress than was Hayes, who sometimes, like Jefferson, preferred very casual attire. Hayes did, however, have a valet. His name was Isaiah E. Lancaster, and he began to work for the future President about 1873. He served throughout the presidency of Hayes, and also accompanied the Chief Executive on the celebrated Great Western Tour of 1880.

The direct association of Hayes and Arthur is a curious tale. Hayes' dismissal of Arthur from the New York Customhouse post apparently did not engender lasting hatred, nor did it keep the two Presidents apart in later life. Hayes and Arthur shared a private carriage in the Grant funeral procession. Hayes confided to his diary: "President Arthur proved an excellent companion for such a drive—five hours." The following year Hayes attended Arthur's funeral, and he was requested by the Arthur family to be a pallbearer. Actually he and President Cleveland rode with the mourners.[6]

Other comparisons and contrasts between Arthur and Hayes suggest themselves. Both men had a Vermont connection, Arthur by birth, and Hayes by ancestry. Both were good students and won election to Phi Beta Kappa, Arthur in course at Union, and Hayes at Kenyon as a distinguished alumnus and valedictorian of his class. Both men practiced law and participated in some unusual cases which earned them recognition at the bar.

Neither man really sought the presidency, or a second term.[7] Both owned handsome Brewster carriages, and both traveled widely throughout the United States when it was far less common for Presidents to do this than today. Arthur made trips to both Florida and Yellowstone National Park in 1883. Hayes also made a Southern tour, and later undertook the first visit by a President, in office, to the West Coast.

Each man entered the White House under a cloud—Hayes the

victim of America's strangest presidential election; Arthur the unwitting benefactor of the Garfield tragedy. Each worked under the handicap of factionalism within his party, and each lacked a clear mandate from the electorate. Each President overcame or modified these obstacles.

There are some important differences, too, between Arthur and Hayes. Although both were large men, the former was much taller. Arthur stood six feet two inches and once weighed 250 pounds; Hayes was fairly short at five feet eight inches, but his weight reached 192 pounds while he was President, and he possessed a powerful torso and a large head. Arthur had full side whiskers and a moustache; Hayes preferred a full beard. The Ohioan enjoyed excellent health throughout his life. Arthur contracted kidney disease and his health was impaired several times during his presidency, before he finally succumbed to Bright's disease, and other complications, in November 1886. Arthur was also sick during Garfield's incapacity at a time when the United States lacked a President *pro tempore* of the Senate and a Speaker of the House of Representatives.[8]

The family situation of the two Presidents is also in sharp contrast. Hayes was extremely fortunate. Probably no statesman of his time enjoyed a happier marriage or closer family ties. He had five children, including three grown sons, one of whom, Webb, acted as his father's confidential secretary and sometime bodyguard. Arthur lost his wife, Ellen, in death shortly before he became Vice-president; his grief was never fully assuaged. Perhaps these family differences help to explain why Hayes liked his role as President better than Arthur. Hayes accepted the job with a note of humor despite his singular victory. About three days after his inauguration, he wanted to go out for a walk, and discovered there was but one door to the White House, the front one. So he went out that door, only to find a large crowd, through which he forced his way. "It's almost as much trouble to get out of this house as it is to get into it," he said laughingly, referring, of course, to his fight for the position.[9]

Usually a President and his Vice-president go their own way in line of duty and see little of each other. Arthur even worked at cross-purposes with Garfield. Hayes and Wheeler, however, were very friendly, and the Vice-president from New York was frequently a social visitor at the White House, especially on Sunday evenings.

Professor Reeves concludes his paper by observing that Arthur fitted the needs of his time and "calmed a nation jolted by assassination" for the second time in 16 years. In the same sense Hayes calmed a nation after the bitterness of the Civil War and Reconstruction. Both administrations were markedly free of corruption, and both promoted business. Each of these Gilded Age Presidents understood his situation perfectly, and performed well in the nation's highest office.

Grover Cleveland:
Revitalization of the Presidency

Vincent P. De Santis

It has become a historical convention to represent Grover Cleveland's presidency as the most distinguished one between that of Lincoln and Theodore Roosevelt. According to the influential and widely used American history textbook by Samuel Eliot Morison, Henry Steele Commager, and William E. Leuchtenburg, "He alone of the titular leaders of either party [of the Gilded Age] had sufficient courage to defy the groups that were using the government for selfish purposes and to risk his career in defense of what he thought was right."[1] Allan Nevins, who has made the most exhaustive study, albeit a favorable one, of Cleveland, associates four achievements with his name. He restored honesty and impartiality to government; he planted deep in the American mind the idea that the evils of the protective tariff system ought to be abolished; he saved the nation from the abandonment of the gold standard at a time when abandonment might have produced economic chaos; and he taught the American people that in their handling of foreign affairs, conscience should always be the one dominant force.[2] Morison, Commager, and Leuchtenburg, seeing Cleveland's achievements in a slightly different way, point out that he advanced civil service reform, challenged the predatory interests that were taking up the public lands of the nation, denounced the evils of protection and dramatized the tariff issue, and called a halt to the raids on the United States Treasury by war veterans and their lobbyists.[3]

Yet Cleveland's reputation in the presidency commonly rests, not so much upon his accomplishments or brilliance, as upon his character. "It is as a strong man, a man of character, that Cleveland will live in history," writes Nevins. "It was his personality, not his mind that made so deep an impress upon his time."⁴ And, according to Richard Hofstadter, Cleveland stood out "if only for honesty and independence, as the sole reasonable facsimile of a major president between Lincoln and Theodore Roosevelt."⁵ Historians have praised Cleveland for his courage, firmness, uprightness, sense of duty, and common sense. They have described him as having a steely stubbornness, of being ruggedly independent, of standing like an oak for his principles, of having the courage to scorn popularity, of rising above the needs of the party and keeping unerringly in view the needs of the country, of not being able to be bought or bullied, and as being the prototype of jut-jawed firmness. Thus the portrait of a fearless and heroic figure hewing to the line developed and, in general, historians have maintained it.

Cleveland, a strapping figure of well over 200 pounds, came to the White House in 1885 with the reputation of a reformer and a man of courage, integrity, and prodigious work habits. Actually, he was unimaginative, obdurate, brutally forthright, and candid. He was also a thoroughgoing conservative, a believer in sound money, and a defender of property rights. In his Inaugural Address he promised to adhere to "business principles," and his Cabinet included conservatives and business-minded Democrats. His administration indicated no significant break with his Republican predecessors on fundamental issues. Yet he appealed to Americans, because he seemed to be a plain man of the people and because he consistently appeared to do what he believed to be right. The public admired him for what was called his "you be damnedness," and it loved him for the enemies he had made. Cleveland was plainspoken. If he thought a proposition was a steal he said so. A robber, a thief, a sneak, a liar, and a cheat had no euphemistic titles in the lexicon of Cleveland's veto messages. Naturally the people were pleased.

And Cleveland has proved attractive to historians. In two polls on presidential greatness conducted by Arthur M. Schlesinger in

1948 and 1962, Cleveland was rated one of America's ten greatest Presidents. He was placed in the near-great category on both
occasions, being number eight on the first poll and number ten
on the second. Why he dropped two notches in the interval between polls is not clear, but Thomas Bailey says the explanation
for this may have been "that by 1962 the bloom had worn off" of
Nevins' admiring biography of Cleveland and that "perhaps
the 19th century rugged individualism of stubborn Old Grover
did not fit into the hope-freighted atmosphere of Kennedy's New
Frontier."[6] Cleveland achieved Near Greatness in these polls, according to Schlesinger, because of his stubborn championship of
tariff reform and of honesty and efficiency in the civil service.
(See Appendix.)

In an extension of the Schlesinger polls, a University of Kansas sociologist polled in a random way the membership of the Organization of American Historians on an evaluation of Presidents
and published his findings in 1970. Overall Cleveland did well,
being rated between 12th and 14th among the Presidents in general prestige, strength of action, activeness, idealism, and accomplishments. Only on the matter of flexibility did Cleveland receive
a low rating—27th among the Presidents.[7] But this only served to
strengthen the belief about one of the great sides of his character—his unyielding determination.

Cleveland was President during a period when politics and
politicians were under a harsh indictment by thoughtful observers. "No period so thoroughly ordinary has been known in American politics since Christopher Columbus first disturbed the balance of power in American society," commented Henry Adams.

One might search the whole list of Congress, Judiciary, and
Executive during the twenty-five years from 1870 to 1895 and
find little but damaged reputation. The period was poor in
purpose and barren in results. . . .

"Even among the most powerful men on that generation," Adams
resumed later, speaking of the politicians, there was "none who
had a good word for it."[8] Lord Bryce believed the major parties

GROVER CLEVELAND
March 18, 1837–June 24, 1908
The Twenty-second and Twenty-fourth President of
The United States

were in danger of losing their functional usefulness, because they failed to offer the electorate an opportunity to vote on issues, and because they used public office to reward party workers. "Neither party has any principles, any distinctive tenets," charged Bryce. They "were like two bottles. Each bore a label denoting the kind of liquor it contained, but each was empty."[9]

While historians today have the benefit of more sources and perspective than Adams and Bryce, they have in the main accepted those contemporary judgments. In fact many historians have competed with one another to find suitable disparaging phrases to censure the politics of the Gilded Age. Most historians believe that at no other time in American history was the moral and intellectual tone of political life so uniformly low nor were political contests so preoccupied with patronage. "There is no drearier chapter in American political history," Morison, Commager, and Leuchtenburg tell us. "National politics became little more than a contest for power between rival parties waged on no higher plans than a struggle for traffic between rival railroads."[10]

Cleveland was President also during a period when the presidency was at a low ebb in power and prestige and when national political power was largely vested in Congress. Congressional leaders had nearly overthrown Andrew Johnson, gained almost complete control of Grant, and tried to put their successors in the Gilded Age at their mercy. In these years the Whig theory of the presidency prevailed, which held that the President must confine himself to the execution of laws enacted by an omniscient Congress. Senator John Sherman, Republican leader of Ohio, and a longtime aspirant to the White House, expressed this view when he wrote, "The executive department of a republic like ours should be subordinate to the legislative department. The President should obey and enforce the laws, leaving to the people the duty of correcting any errors committed by their representatives in Congress." Congressional leaders acted on these principles. "The most eminent Senators," wrote George F. Hoar of Massachusetts about his colleagues in the Senate, "would have received as a personal affront a private message from the White House expressing a desire that they should adopt any course in the discharge of their legislative duties that they did not approve. If they visited the White House, it was to give, not receive advice." Henry Adams agreed, noting, "So far as the President's initiative was concerned, the President and his Cabinet might equally well have departed separately or together to distant lands."[11]

Despite his solid personal qualities, Cleveland's presidency was largely a negative one. "He was too conservative to be a great constructive statesman," writes Nevins.[12] For the most part he seemed unable to comprehend the far-reaching economic and social changes accompanying the rise of industrialism and urbanism in his day. Or, when he revealed an awareness of what they amounted to, as he did in his annual message of 1888, he was slow or reluctant to do much about them. In that message Cleveland pointed out that,

> . . . the fortunes realized by our manufacturers are no longer solely the reward of sturdy industry and enlightened foresight, but they result from the discriminating favor of the Government and are largely built upon undue exactions from the masses of our people. The gulf between employers and the employed is constantly widening, and classes are rapidly forming, one comprising the very rich and powerful, while in another are found the toiling poor. . . .
>
> Corporations, which should be carefully restrained creatures of the law and the servants of the people, are fast becoming the people's masters.[13]

Though Cleveland was a Democrat, he fully shared the Whig-Republican view of the extent of federal power and the role of the President in domestic matters. These did not extend to the maintenance of prosperity nor to the increase of well-being, and they did not include the responsibility for avoiding or ameliorating conditions which precipitated social and labor disturbances in the 1890s. Because he firmly opposed what he called paternalism, Cleveland was not sympathetic with the problems and protests of the nation's farmers and workers when the country was afflicted during his second term with the most severe depression it had yet seen. Cleveland was, in fact, an incredibly simple man to have been President toward the end of the nineteenth century, concludes Rexford G. Tugwell who writes about him that "he was as innocent as a child of the large thoughts a statesman must have had about his nation's position in the world," and "he probably had never considered, either, the role of government in an industrialized society."[14]

Cleveland strongly opposed the idea of the government giving aid to anyone in distress, and his political philosophy in this respect is best illustrated in his veto of the Texas Seed bill early in 1887. Certain Texas counties suffering from a drought were in pressing need for seed grain. In response to the pleas of a number of sufferers Congress passed a bill appropriating $10,000 to enable the Commissioner of Agriculture to distribute seed. The amount was trivial, but the measure sharply challenged Cleveland's belief. He had just vetoed the Dependent Pensions bill, and he regarded the Texas Seed bill in the same light. He returned the measure unsigned with a strong protest, because he believed it was wrong "to indulge a benevolent and charitable sentiment through the appropriation of public funds for that purpose." He went on to say he could "find no warrant for such an appropriation in the Constitution, and I do not believe that the power and duty of the General Government ought to be extended to the relief of individual suffering which is in no manner properly related to the public service or benefit." Then he added significantly: "A prevalent tendency to disregard the limited mission of this power and duty should, I think, be steadfastly resisted, to the end that the lesson should be constantly enforced that though the people support the Government the Government should not support the people."

In other phrases of this memorable veto, which have been quoted again and again in behalf of the same philosophy, Cleveland reminded Americans that "Federal aid in such cases encourages the expectation of paternal care on the part of the Government and weakens the sturdiness of our national character. . . ." In his Second Inaugural Address in 1893, Cleveland returned to this theme when he dwelt at length on the "unwholesome prog-

eny of paternalism" and when he complacently added, "The lessons of paternalism ought to be unlearned and the better lesson
taught that while the people should patriotically and cheerfully
support their Government its functions do not include the support of the people."[15]

In Cleveland's opinion Americans were entitled to economy,
purity, and justice in their government, and nothing more. There
was to be a fair field for all and favors for none. One of Cleveland's conceptions of his role as President was that of a righteous
watchdog whose business it was to look after other politicians
and to prevent them from giving and taking favors. Thus, he
opposed tariff favors to business, pension favors to veterans,
and land favors to railroads. Cleveland's two terms of obstruction mark his place in history as a largely negative President,
who believed it was his duty to prevent bad things from occurring, and not to make good things happen.

But not all effective leadership is of a positive nature, con-
tends Thomas Bailey about presidential greatness, even though
the constructive leader is generally praised more than the obstructive one. Bailey commends Cleveland for his stiff-necked
determination not to be stampeded by Congress into a clash
with Spain over atrocities in Cuba. When a bellicose congressman reminded him that the Constitution authorized Congress to
declare war, Cleveland rejoined, "Yes, but it also makes me the
Commander-in-Chief, and I will not mobilize the army." "Sheer
negativism," adds Bailey, "or the ability to put one's foot down
when it ought to be put down is often commendable in a
leader."[16]

Cleveland's shining hour, argues Louis W. Koenig, occurred
"in the assertion of principle . . . against the test of events."
Horace Samuel Merrill thinks "Cleveland was much more successful as a defender of the status quo than as a crusader for
peace," and Tugwell is of the opinion that Cleveland "was not
a leader; he was a caretaker."[17] Then, of course, there is Nevins,
who relates how Cleveland "under the heaviest attacks, and wildest abuse, with few to aid or defend him, still smote the desk
with his fist and cried, 'Never, never.'" To have bequeathed a

nation "such an example of iron fortitude," continues Nevins, "is better than to have swayed parliaments or to have won battles or to have annexed provinces." In fact, says Nevins, Cleveland's greatest service to the country was to leave to subsequent generations an example of "courage that never yields an inch in the cause of truth and that never surrenders an iota of principle to expediency."[18] This view of Cleveland has not substantially changed. For as Morison, Commager, and Leuchtenburg conclude about Cleveland, "If the total achievements of his administration were negative, even that was something of a virtue at a time when too many politicians were saying 'yes' to the wrong things."[19]

When Cleveland took office he knew little or nothing about being President and about the great national issues of his day. He intended, he said, to have around him the best minds which shun extravagance and waste. In his First Inaugural Address he declared, "The people demand reform in the administration of the Government, and the application of business principles to public affairs."[20] And as Cleveland began the actual work of being President it was clear that he meant to keep the words of his inaugural. Practically ignoring the matter of legislation, Cleveland spent just about all his time at his first Cabinet meeting and most of his time at the next six meetings discussing departmental reforms.

Cleveland had no inner group of counselors who had accompanied his progression from Buffalo to Albany to Washington. Daniel Lamont had been his private secretary as governor and came to Washington to serve the President in the same capacity, until Cleveland made him Secretary of War in the second administration. Lamont was necessary as a political adviser, although the President also relied heavily upon the counsel of Daniel Manning and William C. Whitney, who headed the Treasury and Navy departments respectively.

There was little staff assistance at the White House executive office in Cleveland's day to help the President with major policy matters. There was no brain trust to supply the President with ideas and to provide him with a friendly opposition. Neither was there a group of administrative assistants to put his ideas into form and to do important tasks. To remedy this situation Cleveland considered naming William L. Wilson, who had served both in the Cabinet and the House of Representatives, as Assistant to the President at a salary of $10,000 a year. When Cleveland could find no appropriation he gave up the idea, but not before he had considered paying Wilson out of his own pocket.

Another major difficulty for Cleveland, particularly in handling public opinion, was his inability to get along with the press. Urged to invite friendly editors and publishers to dinner, he refused on the ground that he should not make himself "familiar with them" simply because they were personally agreeable. Neither was he much more cordial to reporters and correspondents. Still, he regarded this liability of temperament as an asset, claiming that efforts to create a censorship of the press had never received any encouragement from him. Cleveland did not realize that Americans were developing a greater interest in the personal aspects of the presidency. He was a prime target for journalistic censure and ridicule. When he did not go fishing on Memorial Day, he was accused of insulting the memory of the Union dead. Editors pretended that his speeches were plagiarized from an encyclopedia, or written for him by his "over-educated sister." Cleveland retaliated by sending angry letters to editors. And at a banquet to celebrate Harvard's 250th anniversary, he denounced the "silly, mean, and cowardly lies that . . . are found in the columns of certain newspapers, which violate every instinct of American manliness, and in ghoulish glee desecrate every sacred relation of private life." No wonder then that Ambrose Bierce should have defined the presidency in his *Devil's Dictionary* as "the greased pig in the field game of American politics."[21]

In his relations with Congress, Cleveland made little effort to bring the political branches of the government into an effective unit. In fact, in his first years of office, he was one of the least inclined of all Presidents to quarrel with Congress over a matter of power. Cleveland had great reverence for the doctrine of separate powers, and his favorite political theme for a while was the "Independence of the Executive." This view, however, caused him trouble, and in the end he had to give it up. But his reluctance to interfere with Congress was the despair of his friends. William L. Wilson, quite disappointed by the outcome of the Wilson-Gorman Tariff of 1894, confided to his diary that Cleveland was "woefully lacking in the tact of making ordinary men and especially representative public men feel a personal relationship and a personal loyalty to him by little social and conventional attentions. Always courteous, frequently kindly, always frank and business-like he yet did not seem to think of the power he had and possibly the duty he was under, to tie men to him by personal ties, rather than by political or business relations." Wilson believed that Cleveland could have kept many members of Congress personally friendly "by a casual invitation to lunch, or a formal invitation to dinner, a stroll together or a carriage drive." In the opinion of Woodrow Wilson, Cleveland "thought it no part of his proper function to press his preference in any other way [than by recommendation in a message] upon the acceptance of Congress. . . . But he deemed his duty done when he had thus used the only initiative given him by the Constitution and expressly declined to use any other means of pressing his views on the party. He meant to be aloof, and to be President with a certain separateness as the Constitution seemed to suggest."[22]

Like other Chief Executives, Cleveland had his own conception of the presidency. His view of the office was largely influenced by his sense of responsibility and uprightness and by his conservatism. Thus his conception was both strong and weak. The President should do all he possibly could to assure the national good but without encroaching upon or pushing the legislative or judicial branches of government. He would not pursue social adventures, but if order or security were threatened he would take action against disturbers and aggressors. Cleveland firmly believed in the doctrine of the separation of powers and regarded the presidency as "essentially executive in nature." Furthermore he believed the most important benefit he could confer on the country by his presidency was "to insist upon the entire independence of the Executive and legislative branches of the government and to compel the members of the legislative branch to see that they have responsibilities of their own."[23] And while Cleveland viewed the presidency as "pre-eminently the people's office," he also regarded it as one in which he had the duty to exercise all his powers to protect the interests of the federal government.[24]

Cleveland's view of the presidency could be described as a mixed or combined view—insisting upon the independence of the different branches of government, yet holding to the idea of a strong executive and of government for the people preeminently. This is why he is sometimes called "A Third Kind of President"—one moving between the strong concept exemplified by Lincoln and the weak concept represented by Buchanan. According to Sydney Hyman, the Cleveland presidency shuttled between these two concepts of the presidency. "Now it seems to say the Presidential office is chiefly an administrative one; now it seems to say it is also a political one," writes Hyman. "Now it talks of leading a march toward brave new horizons; now it draws back from adventure. Now it seems prepared to follow the lead of the Congress; now it seems disposed to tell the Congress to mind its own business and to keep its nose out of Executive business." But Hyman concludes that the distinctive trait in the Cleveland concept of the presidency is that the essential presidential function lies in defensive directions. It lies in veto, in disengagement, in the negation of what others have put in motion, or in the use of only enough executive energy to maintain an existing equilibrium.[25]

Cleveland's belief in a hands-off attitude on his part toward legislation was in line with the prevalent view in the Gilded Age that the President should not attempt to shape legislation or meddle in the affairs of Congress. He did not begin to influence the form of legislation until about halfway through his first term, and he did not follow through on legislation. In his second term he leaned more toward the view that the President should help push laws through, and his efforts in behalf of the repeal of the Sherman Silver Purchase Act in 1893 indicate this change. But Cleveland's leadership in this instance was in behalf of negative rather than positive action. Though he had said that "the administration must be ready with some excellent substitute for the Sherman Law," he failed to offer any constructive alternative. And he continued to hold the view that the President should work independently of the legislative branch if this could be done.

At times Cleveland's different views about the presidency clashed and were tested under provocation, when Cleveland acted more like a strong President than a weak one. He faced no crisis of the magnitude that confronted Jackson, Buchanan, and Lincoln, but on two important occasions, the Pullman strike and the Venezuelan boundary dispute, he was not reluctant to expand the powers of the presidency. As Lincoln was called on to preserve the Union, says Tugwell, "Cleveland was asked to preserve order and to ensure the national influence in the Western Hemisphere."[26] Perhaps Cleveland's views of the presidency were also tested but found wanting in the problems created by the new industrialized society in America, especially during the depression of his second term.

In his First Inaugural Address Cleveland stressed such words as "responsibility," "conscience," and "duty," and these became important aspects of the tone and style of his presidency. This is clearly demonstrated by the long hours and hard work he put in, working until two or three in the morning, personally taking care of his own correspondence (he never used stenographers), and answering all White House telephone calls in person. It is also demonstrated by his meticulous attention to details such as the scrutiny and veto of private pension bills for Civil War veterans and his compulsion to do just about everything himself, including minor tasks that a mere clerk could have handled. He was probably the hardest-worked man in Washington in his day, and his attention to details was often considered more a fault than a virtue. Samuel Tilden observed that "he would rather do something badly for himself than have somebody else do it well."[27] Performing most of these tasks himself made it difficult for Cleveland to give the attention he should have given to some of the larger issues. And his critics complained that it would have been better for him to go to bed for a good night's sleep and then face the big problems the next day with a clear brain.

Honesty also pervaded Cleveland's style and tone. He worked to keep both major and minor matters honest, and William Allen White says, "It was all honest."[28] For example he insisted on paying himself for the hay supplied by the government in the barn set aside at the White House for the President's private use.[29] And when Cleveland went on vacation he paid his own expenses.

An unswerving loyalty to duty also characterized Cleveland's presidency, but it made it nearly impossible for him to compromise. He seemed unable to meet agreeably with those who differed with him. He was suspicious of them and likely to denounce them personally. What is now called Cleveland courage was in his own day known in Washington in many quarters as obstinacy.

"Few presidents," writes Wilfred E. Binkley, "have ignored pressures to the extent that Cleveland did or paid as heavy a penalty for it."[30] A prime example is his annual message to Congress of December 1887, all of which he devoted to a demand for reduction of the tariff. He had been strongly advised not to touch the tariff or to make an issue of it in the presidential campaign of 1888. But he believed it was his duty to do something about the tariff, and he was so immovable on his decision that he told John G. Carlisle, Speaker of the House, "If every other man in the country abandons the issue, I shall stick to it."[31] While Cleveland's tariff message pleased reformers, it was criticized as bad politics by many Democratic politicians. Raising the tariff issue just then gave the protectionists an opportunity to exploit some of the emotional issues going back to the Civil War. And, whether correctly or not, many observers then and since have attributed Cleveland's defeat in 1888, followed by the enactment of the highest tariff in our history, the McKinley Tariff of 1890, to Cleveland's stubborn and candid handling of the tariff issue. Cleveland's impact on the presidency was felt and evidenced in other ways. He was really the first President to use the veto freely. Presidents before Cleveland had used the veto sparingly. Washington had vetoed two bills only, and his successors down to 1830 had returned seven to Congress. Jackson made a bolder use of his power—12 vetoes—that aroused intense opposition. Yet until the accession of Cleveland in 1885, the total number of bills vetoed was only 132, including the pocket vetoes, in 96 years. Cleveland vetoed 301 bills in his first term, most of them private pension measures, but on occasion he vetoed an important matter such as an act restricting Chinese immigration.

Cleveland's most notable impact on the presidency was his successful effort to restore the powers and initiative of the Chief Executive largely lost by Johnson in his fight with Congress during Reconstruction. There were some stirrings of presidential assertion against congressional aggression in the years between Johnson and Cleveland, and there had been some presidential victories, particularly on the part of Hayes and Garfield. But the Tenure of Office Act remained to harass Presidents. Cleveland made a major contribution to the strengthening of the presidency, not only by reasserting his prerogatives and refusing to relinquish them, but also by bringing to an end the Tenure of Office Act and its protracted aggression upon the presidency. In this spectacular contest with the Senate, Cleveland gained both a personal and a political victory, and the legislative branch was pushed out of disputed ground within the executive enclave. This reversal of Republican theory and practice was the most important gain for the presidency in the post-Civil War years.

Cleveland helped to strengthen the presidency also by his action in the controversy with Britain over Venezuela. He did this by bringing into the presidential arena all negotiations with another country and keeping there the initiative of their conduct. He later told a friend that his "aim was at one sharp stroke to bring the whole matter into his own hands, compel England to yield to arbitration, and put Congress in a position where it could not interfere. . . ." In doing this, Tugwell argues, Cleveland "ad-

vanced the Presidency immensely by foreclosing the leadership
in foreign affairs which might have escaped him if he had tem-
porized."[32]

In addition to advancing the presidency, Cleveland exceeded its limits and introduced a new pattern of the use of
the military in civil disorder when he used the Army to "restore law and order" in the Pullman strike of 1894, over the
opposition of the governor of Illinois, John P. Altgeld. And,
since Cleveland was a lawyer, it can be assumed he was
fully aware of his constitutional offense. Cleveland never con-
sulted Altgeld as to the necessity for federal interference
but instead relied on Attorney General Richard Olney, who
considered that interference with the mails made it necessary for the President to see that the laws were faithfully
executed. Some historians believe that, in the decision
Cleveland made in the Pullman strike, he was "unduly influenced" by Olney, "a tough-fisted and ultra-conservative
Cabinet member," and that, in the Venezuelan boundary
dispute, "Cleveland had allowed Olney to take him far on
the road to war."[33]

Finally, it is significant to note the change in view that a
future President had about the office after living through
Cleveland's presidency. Woodrow Wilson, in his critique of
the American system in his *Congressional Government*
(1885), after observing the Presidents from Johnson through
Arthur, concluded there was no hope in the presidency and
that congressional supremacy would have to be recognized
and that body would have to accept the responsibilities of
leadership. But, after observing Cleveland in action, Wilson
altered his view. In approving the President's conduct, he
said it had been direct, fearless, and practical, and that it
had "refreshed our notion of an American Chief Magistrate." Wilson noted that Cleveland had changed while in
office from a President who had considered himself to be responsible only for administration to one who had risen to the
challenge and had become what a President should be—a
policy-maker and a shaper of opinion. Wilson praised Cleve-

land as the only President between 1865 and 1898 who "played a leading and decisive part in the quiet drama of our national life."[34]

"By most meaningful tests Grover Cleveland, though an outstanding character, was not an outstanding President," concludes Thomas Bailey in his study of *Presidential Greatness*. He was too provincial and narrow-visioned. Furthermore, he was not in tune with his times, for he "never fully grasped the significance of the vast social and economic changes that were convulsing the country."[35] There is some merit in this assessment. Cleveland acted more as an overseer than as an initiator or organizer. He preferred to have things come to him rather than to propose or push them through Congress. Yet he is generally rated as one of the ablest Presidents. This is because he showed a degree of independence and courage that is rare in public life. Fidelity to the law and to duty enhanced Cleveland's reputation as a President who stopped things rather than started them. He checked abuses, he restrained bad men from carrying out their schemes, he warded off impending calamity, and he stopped foreign aggrandizement in the Western Hemisphere. He will be remembered always as one who every hour of the working day did what he thought was right. And Cleveland performed his task so well that for his generation and later ones as well he became the embodiment of this kind of presidential action. This is why Hofstadter can call him "the flower of American political culture in the Gilded Age."[36]

The Vindication of an Idol

Mark D. Hirsch

I COME NOT TO bury Grover Cleveland but to praise him! When I first received Professor De Santis' paper, I read it with a sense of ominous foreboding. He had started: "It has become a historical convention to represent Grover Cleveland's presidency as the most distinguished one between that of Lincoln and Theodore Roosevelt," and with some trepidation I expected an expression of critical revisionism damaging to Cleveland's reputation and to the customary favorable interpretation of his record. As a student of Allan Nevins', I must confess to you that Cleveland was my god, and Nevins was his high priest. I had developed a high regard for this President. In 1932, prior to the publication of his Pulitzer Prize-winning biography, Professor Nevins had asked me to check every single fact and footnote in the text, where possible, and as a result I had come to know this President well. Moreover, two seminars concentrating upon his two administrations, a master's thesis dealing with the repeal of the Tenure of Office Act, and a doctorate that was a biography of a close associate, William C. Whitney, had only fortified my deep admiration for Cleveland.

You can therefore imagine my apprehension as I began to examine Professor De Santis' critique. But as I read the first three pages, a metamorphosis came over me. My dread turned into pleasure, my fears fell away, and I quickly became aware of an unexpected phenomenon: he was really—albeit unwittingly—praising Grover Cleveland rather than enlarging upon his deficiencies and calling for a stark reappraisal of his character and record! It was with rare good humor that I read of Cleveland's four achievements: 1. "He restored honesty and impartiality to government"; 2. he made Americans conscious of the idea "that the evils of the [then] protective tariff system ought to be abolished"; 3. "he saved the nation from the abandonment of the gold standard" at a time when this would have proven economically chaotic; and 4. he had taught the American people that "conscience should always be the one dominant force" in their conduct of foreign affairs (an unusual lesson that many say is so urgently needed again today).

Professor De Santis then cites Morison, Commager, and Leuchtenberg as recognizing Cleveland's additional achievements from a different perspective, namely that "he advanced civil service reform, challenged the predatory interests that were taking up the public lands of the nation [another Tiberius Gracchus?], . . . and called a halt to the raids on the United States Treasury by war veterans and their lobbyists." De Santis further concedes that the President's reputation rests not so much upon accomplishments or brilliance, as upon "character." He notes that according to Richard Hofstadter, Cleveland stood out for "honesty and independence" as the only major President between Lincoln and Theodore Roosevelt. Professor De Santis observes that historians have praised Cleveland for his "courage, firmness, uprightness, sense of duty, and common sense"; that he had a "steely stubbornness," was "ruggedly independent," stood "like an oak for his principles," that he could not "be bought or bullied," and that he had a "jut-jawed firmness"! He then adds the elder Professor Schlesinger's verdict of near-greatness and a new Cleveland quality: "efficiency in the civil service"—based upon two polls taken in 1948 and 1962.

But De Santis gets down to the nub of his thesis by charging Cleveland with being stolid, unimaginative, and stubborn. Furthermore he cites a 1970 poll at the University of Kansas taken among the Organization of American Historians in which Cleveland placed between 12th and 14th in presidential greatness in the areas of general prestige, strength of action, activeness, idealism, and accomplishments. In flexibility, he ranked 27th—but, as De Santis admits, this could actually be a tribute to "his unyielding determination." When he cites Bryce and Adams, they and other critics of the Gilded Age are simply describing in another way why Grover Cleveland was so attractive to the voters of his time. In truth, this President represented the very opposite of so much of the weakness and vacuity of that gauche era.

I submit, in contrast, a corollary: It is easier to understand Cleveland's worth and appeal when one studies the *campaign* of 1884 primarily, and to a lesser degree that of 1892. The contrast with Blaine, especially, was devastating to that candidate. Compare Cleveland's candid and manly behavior in the Maria Halpin affair, for example, with Blaine's shoddy and unforgivable behavior in the Mulligan and Sanborn letters scandals. It was then that the American electorate became impressed with Cleveland's sterling qualities. And De Santis acknowledges Cleveland's repulse of congressional aggrandizement at the expense of the executive branch after the campaign of 1884. Small wonder then that the American people thought of Cleveland as a solid individual and that De Santis also feels impelled to use that same word to describe him.

Moreover, although he charges Cleveland with being "unable to comprehend the far-reaching economic and social changes accompanying the rise of industrialism and urbanism in his day," how many ranking political leaders of that day *did* comprehend those far-reaching changes? Name three! Name two! Cleveland dealt with problems through mechanical or functional approaches, not philosophical or ideological ones. Is it so different even today at 1600 Pennsylvania Avenue? Cleveland's beliefs and qualities were urgent for his own time. In other words, judging Cleveland by present-day standards and against the yardstick of the complexities of modern society is patently unfair. Even Camelot's walls have been breached in less than a decade and constant scholarly probing has revealed some tarnish on that shining young knight's shield. Which President prior to Franklin D. Roosevelt could safely withstand such canons of comparison?

After De Santis criticizes Cleveland for two terms of obstruction and being an almost entirely negative President, he adduces a spate of evidence by other historians commending Cleveland, mainly for the *same* qualities—but positively expressed. And please note also the President's words when warned by a congressman that Congress could declare war on Spain: "Yes, but it [the Constitution] also makes me the Commander-in-Chief, and I will not mobilize the army"! How refreshing a sentiment! Shall we make any invidious comparisons with other Chief Executives who will remain nameless? Finally, when De Santis depicts Cleveland as believing that it was his duty to prevent bad things from occurring, does he realize that he is presenting half of the anthropologist's definition of a priest? Half a priest—that is a higher station than is given to most laymen on earth to attain!

It must be pointed out here in rebuttal of the assertion to the contrary that the President did have a brain trust of sorts. Whitney, Manning, Fairchild, Colonel Lamont, and one or two others played that role, either formally, or during poker games. In the same vein, it must be realized that the President was grievously badgered by a hostile, majority Republican press. He was suspicious of the press with good reason. The case of the vicious innuendoes that Chauncey M. Depew, "Black Jack" John A. Logan, and others launched against the President's young bride underscores this. Flora Payne Whitney had to sail courageously into Logan in the press and deny his charges that the President abused Mrs. Cleveland. Cleveland's desire to protect his independence, even with Democratic editors and publishers, should not be confused with hostility.

When Professor De Santis states that Cleveland "was one of the least inclined of all Presidents to quarrel with Congress over a matter of power," the repeal of the Tenure of Office Act and later of the Sherman Silver-Purchase Act would contradict this. But then there appear additional qualities of Cleveland. "Responsibility," "conscience," and "duty" became "important aspects of the tone and style of his presidency," not to be outdone by this: "Honesty also pervaded Cleveland's style and tone." It is nice to learn about a President, who you think is overrated, that "an unswerving loyalty to duty also characterized

Cleveland's presidency, but it made it nearly impossible for him to compromise." Those who have studied his administrations would caution, yes, to compromise, if it meant to yield.

De Santis himself shows this when he concedes that Cleveland resisted pressures in respect to the tariff in 1888, more than just implicitly so, by his text and quotations. He knew where his duty lay; witness his determined remark to Speaker Carlisle, quoted in the essay. Not only did Cleveland refuse to play it safe on the tariff that year, but he was just as willing to sacrifice the presidency in 1892 for principle. In the latter year, at the famous Victoria Hotel conference, although he needed Tammany Hall's support in order to carry New York City, he declined to listen to entreaties for compromise and pleas to yield and would promise Tammany and Boss Richard Croker no additional patronage in return for that support. It was Croker who yielded! If this is mere stubbornness, make the most of it. More of it is needed in our public men! Compare Cleveland's treatment of Tammany Boss John Kelly with candidate George S. McGovern's treatment of Chicago's Mayor Richard Daley.

On August 11, 1884, presidential nominee Grover Cleveland wrote to Colonel Daniel S. Lamont the following revealing words:

Now this is for you privately. I want to tell you just how I feel. I had rather be beaten in this race than to truckle to [Benjamin F.] Butler or [John] Kelly. I don't want any pledge made for me that will violate my professions or betray and deceive the good people that believe in me. Of course I appreciate my relations to the party and the earnest desire on the part of many good men to win at almost any price. But I cannot forget that a stiff upper lip may be the best means of bringing about a united action nor that if such a thing is not accomplished the chance to win without the element that threatens trouble is only a forlorn one.

Cleveland did not truckle. Kelly's aid in the campaign is dubious. The state was won by only 1149 votes, and with it the election.

But Cleveland had resisted pressure and temptation, and while he had almost lost the presidency he had won universal admiration. His character needs no verbal adornments.

Play a game with me! Take 10 seconds to do it. Conjure up again the Eagleton tragedy and the Salinger mission, and visualize how Grover Cleveland would have handled either. Don't answer! Actually, it is obvious and no reply is really needed. Dear Lord, please send us another stubborn, paternalistic, negative, obstructive man like Grover Cleveland!

Professor De Santis takes note of Cleveland's worthy vetoes, and suddenly the President is performing valuable services in the Tenure of Office Act repeal and the Venezuelan boundary dispute. He is absolutely correct on Olney, who had been a hard-bitten Boston corporation attorney. The Venezuelan and federal mails (Pullman strike) decisions were difficult ones to make, but the President did not quail. At least he got the mails delivered! With the new postal practice of one or two stars on delivery boxes today, I somehow have the feeling of modern Star-Route Frauds!

Finally, please take note of Woodrow Wilson's paean of praise for Cleveland that De Santis cites. The President's conduct had been direct, fearless, and practical; it had "refreshed our notion of an American Chief Magistrate"; Cleveland had become a policy-maker and a shaper of opinion; and Wilson praised Cleveland as the only President between 1865 and 1898 who had "played a leading and decisive part in the quiet drama of our national life." De Santis now recognizes him as a reformer, and his quotation from Hofstadter is Cleveland's crowning glory: He was "the flower of American political culture in the Gilded Age."

Professor De Santis, join the fraternity—and in this day of Women's Lib, the sorority—of Cleveland admirers. They are legion. Grover Thor is securely enthroned in Valhalla, and Allan Nevins is smiling down benignly and indulgently, for you have effectively amended General Bragg's famous slogan: "We love him for the FRIENDS he has made!"

A Biographer Looks Back on
Theodore Roosevelt

William H. Harbaugh

It IS OFTEN said that if Teddy Roosevelt were President today
the Communists would be blown out of Indochina, the welfare
mess would be cleaned up, and the streets would be cleared of
criminals. Less often it is said that if he were President pollution
would be eliminated, the loopholes in the tax laws would be
closed, and dozens of other corporate privileges would be struck
down. Less often still, it is suggested that he would never have
taken the United States into Indochina.

Fortunately for the historian's credibility, if not for his capacity
to entertain and stimulate, it is not his function to speculate. His
primary obligation is and remains the reconstruction of the past
on its own terms. Yet, the historian, hardly less than anyone else,
is the child of his times.

There is no pure history, no total objectivity. The historian
gives his facts greater or lesser meaning, weaves them into one or
another pattern, in accordance with the values, perspective, and
knowledge of his age. He strives not only to describe what was,
but also to delineate those trends and events which bear most
informatively on and offer the most insight into the institutions
and developments of his own times. In part, that is, he engages
in a search for a usable past, or, to use the vernacular of the
moment, in a quest for relevance. (Note the new-found interest
of our generation in rioting in the eighteenth and nineteenth
centuries.)

The question is not whether the historian should or should not do this. If he did not do it, there would be no need for each generation to write its own history, no rationale for a volume of this sort; in the absence of new perceptions, the histories and biographies of past masters would stand as definitive statements except, of course, when newly uncovered evidence dictated revision. The real question, therefore, is whether in reconstructing the past partly through the eyes of his own generation the historian does so consciously or unconsciously, fairly or unfairly, perceptively or obtusely.

Despite the enlarged understanding that present-mindedness brings to history, it is freighted with perils. The chief of these in biography is a tendency to tear the subject from his historical context—to present him, or at least judge him, against the biographer's values rather than the values of his own times. Sometimes this is done explicitly, more often implicitly. But, regardless of how it is done, it is a disservice to the subject, to history, and to the reader.

One of the better examples of present-mindedness is the late Howard K. Beale's *Theodore Roosevelt and the Rise of America to World Power*, published in 1956. Beale was a man of pacifist and isolationist, or at least anti-imperialist, sympathies. He subscribed to the view, so resurgent today, that almost the entire Far Eastern policy of the United States, from the acquisition of the Philippines through Pearl Harbor and probably, though I am not sure, the action in Korea, was a disaster. Yet Beale was a true scholar. He had a disciplined historical mind, one that rarely let its judgment of current policy impinge on his respect for the historical record. He consequently produced a book remarkable for its sympathetic appreciation of Roosevelt's skillful conduct of diplomacy—his refusal to bluster in foreign affairs while President, his sensitivity to the limits of American power, his reluctance to commit the nation beyond the point of democratic consensus. In a word, Beale measured Roosevelt by the standards of Roosevelt's times and found him tall.

But he also measured him against his own standards. He did this implicitly through carefully selected quotations that revealed Roosevelt the young war-lover and imperialist in all his

THEODORE ROOSEVELT
October 27, 1858–January 6, 1919
The Twenty-sixth President of The United States

ferocity. And he did it explicitly in a final chapter which appraised Roosevelt from the perspective and values of the 1950s.
The latter appraisal was not flattering. Beale warned that in other
hands Roosevelt's "ability, his understanding of international
problems, his interest in power, his desire to be strong enough
to settle questions by might, his secret, highly personal handling
of foreign affairs might have become dangerous to democracy
and to the peace of the world." He declared that Roosevelt failed
in his most important objectives—creation of "a stable world in
which the great civilized nations would refrain from war upon
one another. . . . Thirty years after his death, with military might
such as his wildest dreams could not have pictured, and with a
navy more powerful than any other, his country had suffered
losses in a battle as great as ever before in its history and was
living armed to the teeth in dread of destruction of her cities in
an atomic war." He concluded on a more conjectural note. "Perhaps Roosevelt and his friends could not have led America along
a different path. In so far, however, as they did influence America's course, they influenced it in a direction that by mid-century
was to bring her face to face with grave dangers. . . . The trouble lay not in [Roosevelt's] abilities, but in his values and in
the setting in which he worked, whether from choice or from
necessity."[1]

Against that background, I turn to an assessment of the
presidency of Theodore Roosevelt.

There was a time, roughly a decade ago, when I thought that
I had answered that charge in full. I had just completed some
800 pages of typescript for a biography of T.R., and I had ap-
pended to them four or five pages of summary comment. The
summary statements read in part:

Long after the rationalizations, the compromises, the in-
fights, the intolerance, and all the rest have been forgotten,
Theodore Roosevelt will be remembered as the first great
President-reformer of the modern industrial era—the first to
concern himself with the judiciary's massive property bias,
with the maldistribution of wealth, and with the subversion of

the democratic process by businessmen and their spokesmen in Congress, the pulpits, and the editorial offices; the first to comprehend the conservation problem in its multiple facets, the first to evolve a broad regulatory program for capital, and the first to encourage, however cautiously, the growth of countervailing labor unions; the first President, in fine, to understand and react constructively to the challenge to existing institutions raised by the technological revolution.[2]

My evaluative comments on Roosevelt and foreign affairs were considerably less glowing. I entered a stricture or two on the affront his militarism and chauvinism gave the human spirit, then rather lamely concluded that he would be respected nonetheless for his constructive achievements as President, among which was the realistic pursuit of peace in a world that he understood better than most.

Two years later, in 1963, I had occasion to revise my book for a paperback edition, and four years after that, in 1967, an opportunity to write a 25-page summary of Roosevelt's career as an introduction to a collection of his writings.[3] In both instances I distinguished rather sharply, as indeed I had done in the original edition of the biography, between the foreign policies Roosevelt advocated when out of the presidential office and those he pursued when in it. My judgment of the former was again essentially negative, that of the latter again largely favorable. After dutifully censuring his Panama policy and his insensitivity toward the Chinese, I concluded: "On most issues he acted with restraint, sensitivity, and an astute appreciation of the national interest and the limits of American power." In particular, I approved his realistic attitude toward Japan, an attitude held by none of his successors through the second Roosevelt.[4]

Actually, there was a subtle distinction between my treatment of T.R. and the Far East in the first edition of the biography and in my later writings. It was a distinction that relates directly to the sub-theme of this paper—present-mindedness. Assuredly, the original in 1961 had reflected my realization that the Korean War had tied us inextricably to Chiang Kai-shek and Taiwan and drawn us fatefully into Asia. This was implicit in a passage that noted with implied approval Roosevelt's acquiescence in the strengthening of Japan's suzerainty in Korea in 1905. By 1963— really 1962, for that is when I prepared the paperback revision —two new considerations were weighing on my mind: First, I had come by then to accept the revisionist conclusion that the United States could have avoided war against Japan in 1941. (I might add that I continue to believe that the war against Nazi Germany was necessary and proper.) Second, it was clear to me that the Kennedy administration had made commitments in Laos and Vietnam which might well lead to another Korean-type war or worse.

Beale, I concluded, had been right, after all: the entire Far Eastern policy, from the Open Door Notes under McKinley (Roosevelt approved them) to the creation of SEATO under Eisenhower and Dulles, had been a blunder of tragic proportions. I added to the paperback edition two or three paragraphs which drew heavily on Beale. In particular, I emphasized T.R.'s realization, after he left the presidency, that the potential liabilities of our effort to prevent Japan and Russia from closing the commercial door in North China far exceeded the potential commercial advantages to the United States of keeping it open. My key passage follows:

Perceiving the implications of President Taft's "dollar diplomacy," he [Roosevelt] urged him in December, 1910, to abandon commercial ambitions in Manchuria and China in return for Japanese concessions on immigration. "Japan is not rich, her main interests are on the Continent of Asia, . . ." he wrote Taft on December 8. Two weeks later he warned that to wage "a successful war about Manchuria would require a fleet as good as that of England, plus an army as good as that of Germany." He added that although the "open-door" policy in China was an excellent thing. . . , it completely disappears as soon as a powerful nation determines to disregard it, and is willing to run the risk of war rather than forego its intention. . . . Neither Taft nor most of his successors heeded

Roosevelt's advice, and on December 7, 1941, the tragedy played out.[5]

Were I to revise again, I doubt that I would change the thrust of those statements; our Indochina policy from Truman through Nixon, in my judgment, has simply confirmed their appropriateness. However, I would make other changes on the basis of both new research and what I will call a heightened awareness of T.R.'s chauvinistic legacy as exemplified by the values of certain of his successors. Specifically, I would write more pointedly of the stimulus that the Great White Fleet's voyage around the world gave pro-naval elements in Japan and Germany. I would discuss in more depth the long-term implications of the Roosevelt Corollary to the Monroe Doctrine and the intervention in Santo Domingo in 1904–05, though I would retain my relatively sympathetic explanation of the reasons for the formulation of the Corollary. Finally, as the more or less complete child of my times, I would add a paragaraph to the treatment of T.R.'s conduct of foreign affairs in which I would dilate on the long-term implications of his machismo, exaltation of force, and "my country right or wrong" posturing.

In writing my distillation of Roosevelt's thought and policies for the introduction to his writings in 1967, I remained confident that I had captured the essence of his domestic philosophy in the 1961 book. One of my key statements said:

[Roosevelt's was] a social philosophy that placed primary emphasis on what may best be termed the commonweal. At once more than voluntarism and less than statism, it conceived that private and public interest should be harmonized and that organizations and their leaders should . . . pursue socially useful ends. . . . When he preached duty and responsibility . . . it was in the conviction that there could be no enduring government, no advanced civilization, without it. . . . The problem, of course, was to avoid thwarting the individual's egoistic, yet potentially creative, thrust. Roosevelt's solution anticipated the mid-twentieth century welfare state. He would

use government . . . to foster both individual and organiza-
tional fulfillment. . . . [This] meant almost complete acceptance of an evolutionary or open-ended theory of national development. . . .[To quote from T.R.'s first annual message to
Congress]:
When the Constitution was adopted, at the end of the eighteenth century, no human wisdom could foretell the sweeping
changes, alike in industrial and political conditions, which
were to take place at the beginning of the twentieth century.
At that time it was accepted as a matter of course that the
several States were the proper authorities to regulate, so far as
was then necessary, the comparatively insignificant and strictly
localized corporate bodies of the day. The conditions are
wholly different and wholly different action is called for.[6]

Other passages in both the original and revised editions of the
biography asserted that, because Roosevelt conceived of power
as a creative force, he sometimes resented being inhibited by
law. "Few who knew him would challenge [John] Blum's statement that he, especially, 'may have benefited from the limits on
Presidential power which men who understood the problem in
1787 created.' Yet fewer still would deny that his feeling for
power was one of his great sources of strength, or that his compulsion to use it in the public, rather than his private, interest
set him apart from . . . other authoritarian contemporaries in industry and finance."[7]
    As a biographical statement, I think that those passages hold
up. They explain, no doubt inadequately, something of the nature of T.R.'s feeling for power. I must note, however, that they
were counterbalanced—in fact, largely offset or wiped out—by
numerous other passages which described with implied approval
Roosevelt's frequent defiance of Congress. I recall vividly the
relish with which I quoted T.R.'s account of how he and Gifford
Pinchot outwitted the special interests in the Senate in creating
sixteen million acres of new forest preserves in 1907: " 'The opponents of the forest service turned handsprings in their wrath,
and dire were their threats against the Executive; but the threats

could not be carried out, and were really only a tribute to the efficiency of our action.' "⁸

Such a glorification of presidential power, no matter how noble the end to which the power was directed, is today passé. Almost within one decade John F. Kennedy supported an invasion of Cuba, Lyndon B. Johnson converted the civil war in Vietnam into an American crusade, Richard M. Nixon rained more bombs on Indochina than were dropped on Nazi Germany, and the same President transformed the doctrine of executive privilege into a cover for the concealment of political crimes. As historians and political scientists reflect on such exercises of power unrestrained, they lean increasingly toward the view expressed by Senator George McGovern in his address at Oxford University on January 21, 1973:

> Only a few years ago, liberal scholarship still celebrated the strong executive and sought to strengthen it even more. Now we have learned that the presidency, too, is a neutral instrument, that power in the White House can be abused as well as used—that a reactionary or war-maker can also read Richard Neustadt and James McGregor Burns.⁹

I find that I too lean toward this revisionist position on power, but with some reservations. My easy acceptance of the growth of executive power under Theodore Roosevelt reflected two compelling considerations. First, Congress during the Roosevelt era was a shockingly unrepresentative institution. At that time, the Senate was elected by state legislatures. Most legislatures were gerrymandered in favor of conservative rural interests. Within all but the most purely agricultural states, the rural legislators were controlled by corporate and other business interests; and even within the strictly agricultural states, the railroad and emerging agri-business interests were often dominant. This, of course, explained why states like Wisconsin and Iowa were so long represented in the United States Senate by business spokesmen such as John C. Spooner and William B. Allison. The anti-democratic nature of Congress was compounded, and still is, by the committee system in both houses. It seemed to me at the time I wrote, and it seems to me now, that this left Roosevelt—the guardian of all the people's interest, as it were—little alternative but to circumvent Congress when it was technically within his power to do so, as it was in the case of the forest preserves.

The second consideration was present-mindedness. From 1938 through the revision of the Roosevelt book in 1962, a conservative Republican-Dixiecrat coalition controlled Congress. This coalition was not truly reactionary; it approved piecemeal a good many progressive measures over the years. Yet on balance it thwarted fulfillment of the New and Fair Deals. Equally important was the opposition of the states, then mainly Southern but today also Northern, to implementation of the civil rights program so sweepingly mandated by the federal judiciary and grudgingly enacted by Congress. It was evident in the early 1960s, and it is no less evident in the early 1970s, that such progress as we have made toward extending the most elementary civil and moral rights to minorities has resulted from the centralized power of the federal judiciary and the national executive. So I am still uncertain as to how far I would go in condemning Roosevelt's use of power. Probably I would compromise by elaborating on Beale's and Blum's warnings.

As for Roosevelt's achievements in office, my original conclusion was that T.R. accomplished about all that it was possible to accomplish, given the conservative configuration of power in Congress. I wrote that he had contributed substantially to the evolution of the regulatory state, that he had established a pattern of basing administrative decisions—indeed, public policy as a whole—on the best available scientific evidence, that he had contributed enormously to the nation's future well-being by expanding and dramatizing the role of investigatory commissions. I repeated Robert LaFollette's appraisal of his contribution to the conservation movement: " 'When the historian . . . shall speak of Theodore Roosevelt, he is likely to say . . . that his greatest work was inspiring and actually beginning a world movement for . . . saving for the human race the things on which alone a peaceful, progressive, and happy life can be founded.'" I made numerous other commendatory statements.

Meanwhile, neo-Marxist scholars such as Gabriel Kolko were challenging the central thrust of Roosevelt's program. "Roosevelt," wrote Kolko in 1963 in his *The Triumph of Conservatism*, "never ceased to maintain an incurable confidence that institutional reform could best be obtained by personal transformation of evil doers. . . . [His] separation of 'good' from 'bad' combinations as a means of accepting the major premises of the corporate economy, [was] . . . eminently acceptable to the corporate elite." With great persuasiveness, Kolko went on to argue that Roosevelt's reforms served basically to strengthen, rather than weaken, the dominant capitalistic structure. At the end of the Progressive Era, so he concluded, the distribution of income was essentially unchanged and the real power of the corporate world was greater than ever—because the more sophisticated corporate leaders, working through pliable politicians like Roosevelt, had actually generated major portions of the reform program in their own interests and ridden out other aspects of it. In so doing, they had dissipated, or deflected, popular discontent which might have led to structural reform under genuine reform (i.e., people's) leadership.[10]

All of which, if I read correctly the inferences of Kolko and those who anticipated him and those who followed him, is also to say that the kind of incremental reform the Progressives and their intellectual descendants among the New Dealers, Fair Dealers, and New Frontiersmen stood for—the regulation of industry, the efficient use of human and natural resources, the creation of a welfare state, or as Kolko calls it, a state capitalistic society—were in the last analysis counter-revolutionary. By making the potential dissidents or revolutionaries—that is, the workers and intellectuals—an integral part of the system, they not only forestalled precipitate change, they destroyed any possibility of structural change on an evolutionary basis. Or, to turn it around, they fostered radical change of a conservative rather than progressive kind. This led ultimately, so the theory runs, to the creation of a military-industrial complex which is today sustained at the polls by its working-class members—witness their support of the Indochinese war and of the military-hardware budget. Many other examples, including labor opposition to pollution controls that threaten employment or raise prices, could be adduced.

One could argue, of course, that state capitalism started with the Tariff of 1789 under George Washington and with Alexander Hamilton's Report on Manufacturers in 1791. One could further contend that the canal movement of the 1820s and 1830s or the subsidization of railroads and of manufacturers (through the tariff) under Lincoln was more crucial to the development of state capitalism than the regulatory policies of Theodore Roosevelt. But that would be to beg the immediate question, which is Roosevelt's particular influence.

My own reservations about the Kolko group is not with their ultimate conclusions; we have today, I suspect most of us would agree, a modified form of state capitalism of which the highway and construction industries are as integral a part as the military-industrial complex. It was entirely proper, accordingly, for Kolko, Samuel P. Hays, Robert H. Wiebe, and others to inquire into its origins.[11] I am inclined to think, however, that in the process of that inquiry they allowed their knowledge of the ultimate product to color somewhat their interpretation of original motive, especially T.R.'s. I think, too, that their realization that Roosevelt did indeed share many of the capitalists' basic values led to what I regard as their overly inclusive generalizations on the nature of his program. Certainly T.R. and most other Progressives, including LaFollette, were pro-capitalist. They understood (some more so than others) the need for capital formation, and they perceived the social necessity of increased production. This made them fundamentally sympathetic to many of the capitalists' operational viewpoints, including those on efficiency, large-scale production, and tariff protection. But that hardly means that the ultimate goals of the capitalists and of Roosevelt and his Progressive compatriots were identical. On the contrary, many of them were antithetical.

The corporate world wanted industrial stability and the maximization of profits. Roosevelt wanted the same things, but he wanted them because he deemed them crucial to the general welfare. Admittedly, as Kolko and others have cogently argued, he often backed into reforms. Yet, as I put it in 1961 and would put it again today, significant differences separated T.R. from his conservative friends:

> Roosevelt became morally indignant when confronted with injustice; they remained largely indifferent. Roosevelt would become intellectually involved in the reform itself—in its social and economic merit—and would make it part of his body of affirmative beliefs; they would view it as a necessary evil. Above all else, it was this positive accent that distinguished Roosevelt from his sophisticated conservative consorts, the real proponents of strategic retreat. The President's goal was a better, a more just and less privileged America; theirs, a more ordered America.[12]

The hassle over revision of the anti-trust laws in 1907–08 is illustrative. Many corporation leaders recognized that some revision was desirable, and they supported proposals that would have given them control of the regulatory process. But when Roosevelt threatened to veto any bill that failed to provide for effective regulation, they withdrew their support. As T.R. complained with no little accuracy, the corporations preferred that existing laws be "administered crookedly" rather than that they be revised in the public interest or, indeed, in what sophisticated observers conceived to be the corporations' own long-term interests. The conclusion of the business historian, Arthur Johnson, whom I quoted in my revision of 1963, is still valid: "Whatever his shortcomings, Roosevelt's view of the national interest and the need to keep a balance between the ideal and the reality was broader than that of the groups attempting to influence the pending legislation."[13]

Roosevelt's relations with labor fall into the same general pattern. Until well into the 1960s even liberal non-Marxist historians

tended to downgrade T.R.'s labor policies. His successful intervention in the Anthracite Coal Strike of 1902 was passed off as
politically motivated (the fall elections were in the offing); his
repeated calls for workmen's compensation, minimum-wage and
hours legislation, and all the rest were dismissed as paternalistic.[14] He and most of the other Progressives, it seemed, did
not identify sufficiently with labor. The charge was accurate
enough; Roosevelt had no more confidence that the incipient
labor barons would act responsibly than that corporation leaders
would give the commonweal priority over profits. The course of
events has proved him right, and I would today examine this
point at somewhat greater length than I did originally. I would
also emphasize, as I did not do earlier, that on six separate occasions between 1905 and 1908 Roosevelt sent the Congress special
messages on outlawing the abuse of the injunction in labor dis-
putes. When it is recognized that the injunction was the corporate world's single most effective weapon against the organizing
process, the import of these actions becomes obvious.

I Yet, to insist that the thrust of T.R.'s thought and actions was
sincerely reformist is hardly to answer all the charges leveled by
his critics. To repeat and amplify, those charges are: (1) he
strove to shore up capitalism; (2) he collaborated—by some accounts, colluded—with big business; (3) he undercut the reformers by his attack on muckraking in 1906; (4) he failed to
redistribute wealth; (5) he stimulated the growth of state capitalism through his emphasis on regulation and faith in the benign
character of the regulators; and (6) he undermined the early
civil rights movement.

I I have already responded, however ineffectively, to the first
two of those charges. The third—T.R.'s denunciation of muckraking—hardly warrants comment. He leveled the attack at a
time when he needed conservative support of the Hepburn railroad regulation bill. He coupled it with a demand for federal
supervision of *all* corporations in interstate commerce as well as
a recommendation for a steeply graduated inheritance tax. And
he went on the next year, in a series of extraordinarily radical

messages to Congress, to censure businessmen and their satellites in language that made him the greatest muckraker of them all.[15]

As for the failure to redistribute wealth, the critics are patently correct; there has been no substantial redistribution in this century. A modern reappraisal of Roosevelt and the Progressive Era should emphasize that fact to a greater degree than I did. But it should also make these points: Roosevelt demanded far steeper taxes on war profits in World War I than the Wilson administration was willing to countenance; Roosevelt never dreamed that Congress would make such a mockery of the graduated principle as it has done over the years.

The fifth point has also been discussed in part. Whether by inadvertence or design, T.R. encouraged the growth of state capitalism, and his future biographer will have to grapple with that fact. Again, however, a caveat is warranted. Roosevelt expected that the regulators would be disinterested experts—informed economists and other social scientists—not partisan politicians or representatives of industry. The expectation was never wholly fulfilled. The kind of "collusion" Ralph Nader is constantly unveiling attests to that, as does the pattern of pro-business appointees followed by the Harding, Coolidge, and, most recently, Nixon administrations. Behaviorist historians have meanwhile attacked Roosevelt on the other flank. One of the theses of Samuel P. Hays in numerous articles and Robert H. Wiebe in his *The Search for Order* is that the proliferation of government agencies more or less inspired by Roosevelt created a bureaucratic society in which government became increasingly removed from the people. This is an undeniable truth. Philosophically, moreover, it runs athwart the concept of representative democracy. Yet how, speaking broadly, can it be reconciled with the view that the only way short of socialism that corporate domination of American society could have been prevented was through the creation of truly disinterested regulatory bodies?

I turn finally to Roosevelt and the Negro. I do so with considerable trepidation, for Professor H. S. Merrill, the gentleman who, I trust, will prove to be my distinctly *friendly* critic, has recently treated this topic with considerable perception and understanding. In an important new work, *The Republican Command*, written in collaboration with his wife, Professor Merrill comes out, if I read him fairly, somewhere between the moderately favorable exposition of T.R.'s attitudes toward blacks found in my work and the harshly critical appraisals of the younger historians. I confess at the outset that I would change my treatment substantially were I rewriting today. But first let me comment on my original, and as I now view it, too generous account of Roosevelt's relations with blacks.

In the late 1950s, President Eisenhower's failure to give the nation moral leadership following the school segregation decision of 1954 made Theodore Roosevelt appear to be a paragon of enlightenment. This led me to overestimate Roosevelt's moral leadership a half century earlier. I gave him more credit than he deserved for appointing Negroes to office, and I praised him rather unqualifiedly for denouncing lynching, as he did on several occasions. (I note parenthetically that I was properly distressed by T.R.'s arbitrary dismissal of three companies of black soldiers on unfounded charges, though I continue to believe that that action was more a function of his authoritarian than of his racist strain.) Today, I would recast my passages on Roosevelt and the blacks in this form:

The Square Deal embodied no effort to restore the franchise to Southern blacks, no attempt to legislate against that most heinous of crimes, lynching. Assuredly, Roosevelt believed that discrimination was morally wrong and that a fragmented society could not long flourish. He aspired at one level to bring a minority of blacks into the political process, and he sought at another to make the white South less regional in outlook. But, above all, he wanted to secure his own nomination in 1904 through control of the Southern Republican delegations. To these ends he tried to create a biracial party in the South led by patrician whites and supported by educated blacks. He entered into close relations with Booker T. Washington, and he appointed a number of highly qualified blacks to federal offices in the South. He also invited Washington to dinner at the White House, denounced lynching two or three times, and took federal action against peonage.

Roosevelt's mastery of the Southern Republican machinery came easily. But with the tacit acquiescence of William Jennings Bryan and Alton B. Parker, who was to become the Democratic presidential candidate in 1904, Southern editors and politicians so inflamed the South over "Roosevelt Republicanism" that by the eve of the campaign the enlightened white Southerners around whom the President planned to rebuild the party were reduced to silence. By then, too, the virtual completion of the disfranchisement movement had destroyed the G.O.P.'s potential black constituency and made the notion of a true biracial Republican Party in the South an idle dream.

To make matters worse, Northerners were becoming almost as infected by "scientific" racist theories as Southerners. Progressive Republicans such as Robert M. LaFollette and George W. Norris were indifferent to the race problem. And even Eugene V. Debs forced the Socialist Party executive committee to defer in 1903 to the militantly racist views of one of the party's strongest wings.

Roosevelt subsequently appointed a few more blacks to office and again denounced lynching. But he let several state organizations become "lily white," and made no public statement on the Atlanta race riot of 1906. During the remainder of his presidency the black man hardly figured in his political deliberations. As the Merrills conclude, he simply failed to give the civil rights movement the kind of moral or educational leadership that he gave other causes then unattainable. For, as they also point out in an understanding passage, he allowed the bitter realization, in his words, that fundamentally "the North and the South act in just the same way toward the Negro" to reduce him in the end to inertia. Roosevelt's chosen successor, William Howard Taft, had little interest whatever in the fate of blacks. "I will not be swerved one iota from my policy to the South, . . ." he snapped. "I shall not appoint Negroes to office in the South. . . . I shall not relinquish my hope to build up a decent white man's party there."[16]

A few final words. I continue to believe that, whatever Roosevelt's influence on the development of the corporate state, his contribution to the rise of the welfare state was enormous. I also still believe that his impact on the moral sensibilities of his generation was unique. Were I charged to make yet another revision, I would recount in even greater detail the stimulus T.R.'s pronouncements on domestic issues gave to the great reform movement of the early part of this century. Mowry's description of Roosevelt's influence on the embryonic progressive wing of the California G.O.P. is applicable, it seems to me, to every state in the North. Wrote Mowry:

> His name and his doctrines were grafted into the very origins of the movement, and his position in national affairs was repeatedly used by Californians as an effective answer to the charges of party threats raised against them. . . . He was a source of inspiration, a symbol of progressive virtues, and a protector at the highest court.[17]

I would also include, as I did in the revised edition of 1963, excerpts from a letter New York City's long-term councilman, Stanley M. Isaacs, wrote to me in 1961. "I doubt," said Isaacs, who had kept the faith for four full decades, "if anyone today can realize the personal inspiration that came from direct contact with T.R. or can appreciate the fervor that animated those of us who shared in the early Progressive Party years. T.R. gave us new goals, a broad new purpose—faith in our country's ideals and willingness to press forward along lines we knew to be right." Finally, after commenting at much greater length than before on the the darker, super-patriotic side of the Roosevelt legacy, I would close with this quotation from his writings:

> If on this new continent we merely build another country of great but unjustly divided material prosperity, we shall have done nothing.[18]

Honesty and Integrity, But
Too Much Caution

Horace Samuel Merrill

In CONSIDERING the subject of Theodore Roosevelt, there is so much to say on so many facets of his fantastic career, and so much to say about what other historians have written on the subject, that one scarcely knows where to begin and where to end. Mr. Harbaugh is uniquely qualified for this task. He is the only historian who has successfully caged that "bigger than life" giant between the covers of one volume. Every time I pick up the book, I expect the subject to burst the binding of the book and prance off to hunt lions, chase corporations, pen some colorful rhetoric about his pet so-called "malefactors of great wealth"—Edward H. Harriman and the Standard Oil magnates —or flee to a quiet corner to compose delightful letters to his children.

I venture the guess that, henceforth, a mounting number of historians will attempt, and succeed in writing, meaningful biographies of Roosevelt. They will be able to do so because the present-minded approach Mr. Harbaugh refers to today will make it increasingly easier for them to sift the great mass of material on Theodore Roosevelt. So many important events have taken place since he dominated the stage that it now seems natural to push aside, or greatly condense, numerous details surrounding his career that once seemed to loom so large. Already it seems odd to me that a few years ago a publishing house offered us an entire book on the Great White Fleet that Roosevelt sent around the world. I am less certain than Mr. Harbaugh ap-

125

pears to be that many people are now interested in detailed accounts of Roosevelt's role in foreign affairs. Increasingly, I feel
he emerges as a boyish dabbler in that danger-laden realm.
Less cautious Presidents have since done much more than dab-
ble, and they thereby command more attention from historians
and from readers of the history of foreign relations.

Historians and journalists, however, certainly will continue to
produce special studies that will contain significant and substantial accounts of the views and role of Theodore Roosevelt on
such clearly pertinent subjects as monopoly, race relations, ecol-
ogy, political morality, and public administration. The present-
mindedness Mr. Harbaugh discusses ensures this continuous flow
of Roosevelt literature. Roosevelt had so much to say of interest
on so many matters. Many of these special studies will evolve
out of the continuing popular practice of relating Roosevelt in
one way or another to new interpretations. Such historians as
Gabriel Kolko and John Blum produce accounts that start a
chain reaction of others writing their views on those provocative
interpretations—sometimes to refute their contentions.

Turning more specifically to Mr. Harbaugh's presentation, his
treatment of Roosevelt's legislative record interests me in particular. Mr. Harbaugh says, "My original conclusion was that
T.R. accomplished about all that it was possible to accomplish,
given the conservative configuration of power in Congress."
Whatever might be Mr. Harbaugh's current view of Roosevelt's
legislative record, for my part I emphatically believe that
Roosevelt did not even give it a good try. It seems to me that,
given the great political skill and the popularity with the voters
he supposedly possessed, and the great weakness of the Democratic Party, he did have a very good and a relatively safe opportunity to obtain much more reform legislation. Perhaps
he did not care enough about reform to risk a battle with the
Republican leaders in Congress, or simply failed to appreciate
fully the extent of the need for new legislation. Too, he appeared
to be at a loss as to just what specific changes to propose. Until
he surrendered to his emotions in the fateful 1912 election
campaign, he seemed to be much more interested in maintaining

harmony in the party leadership than he was in achieving reform. He feared the consequences of defeat. Over and over again he expressed a fear of the breakdown of law and order and a suspicion of the masses. Without an elitist control, he was especially fearful that anarchy might prevail, and to him Republican solidarity was the best safeguard against chaos. Moreover, personal pride was doubtless an important factor determining him. He always found it difficult to entertain the thought of personal defeat—especially at the hands of Democrats. So he passed the problems on to the bumbling Taft, his own handpicked bumbler, and Taft passed the golden opportunities to the Democratic Wilson administration. Whatever the reason, or reasons, I repeat, Roosevelt, especially after 1906, failed to give reform legislation a really good try.

Who were the men in Congress who stood in the way of economic reform legislation and seemingly intimidated the sometimes fist-waving Roosevelt? At their fullest strength numerically, they were five in number. In the Senate was the group known as The Senate Four—consisting of Nelson W. Aldrich of Rhode Island, Orville H. Platt of Connecticut, William B. Allison of Iowa, and John C. Spooner of Wisconsin. They controlled both the Senate and the House of Representatives until 1903, when Uncle Joe Cannon became Speaker of the House and obtained a partnership status with The Four in controlling Congress.[1] Roosevelt treated these five men with great deference, and privately sometimes spoke admiringly of them. In March of 1903, he wrote to his friend Taft that he felt respect and regard for them and for a few others in Congress. He added, "They are the leaders, and their great intelligence and power and their desire in the last resort to do what is best for the government, make them not only essential to work with, but desirable to work with."[2]

The only one of these with whom he ever had a clash was Aldrich, and that was but once, and was really minor in nature. It was over the form the Hepburn railroad rate regulation was to take. I say it was minor, because both men, along with almost all the members of Congress, almost all the business community, and the public in general agreed that some federal law on the matter was bound to pass. The disagreement between Roosevelt and Aldrich in that contest ended in such a way that each of them was able to claim it was his own particular victory. Incidentally, it was in the midst of that skirmish that Roosevelt delivered his famous Muckrake Speech that Mr. Harbaugh mentioned. It also was at a time when muckrakers were lambasting without mercy such Senators as Aldrich. It is my guess that Roosevelt delivered the speech in order to assure the Senate leaders that he was not trying to destroy them, but was instead willing to join forces with them to fight off enemies of the Republican organization. He was bidding for party unity at a time when it was important, if the Hepburn bill were to become law in the form he desired.[3]

There are some little publicized examples of Roosevelt's proclivity to pull back from opportunities to engage in actual reform. Why did he not, for example, use his tremendous popularity and oratorical gifts to build up, through the 1906 election, a substantial reform-minded following in Congress? Instead, he urged the election of every candidate with a Republican label, regardless of his views. He allowed his fears of defeat to take command. In August 1906, in a letter to his friend Elihu Root in which he discussed the possible outcome of the 1906 election, Roosevelt stated that "judging from experience of the past the time has about come for the swinging of the pendulum. . . ." But he pointed out, in an apparent effort to brace himself against the impending defeat, that Alexander Hamilton after suffering defeat emerged famous. Roosevelt said, "In Hamilton's few years of public life, which ended by his seeing the actual triumph of the men and the seeming triumph of the principles to which he was most opposed, he nevertheless accomplished an amount of work which has remained vital and effective until the present day."[4] Roosevelt had talked himself into believing that he already had accomplished much.

Of the three major economic issues of the era—the tariff, monopoly, and currency—Roosevelt's record on the tariff was especially unimpressive. True, he did devote considerable time and effort to the question, but he concentrated it all on forestall-

ing congressional consideration of the matter, rather than on revision. He clearly dreaded the thought of getting himself and his
party involved in debate over the tariff. When two of his Cabinet
members exercised in public addresses their proclivity to talk
about the tariff, Roosevelt ordered them to direct their speech-
making to other subjects. One of these men was Secretary of the
Treasury Leslie M. Shaw, an ardent high-protectionist, and the
other was Secretary of War William Howard Taft, a tariff revisionist.[5]

Immediately following the 1904 election, tariff reform newspapers and individuals expressed conviction that Roosevelt would
begin the presidential term with a call for tariff legislation. He
did not include mention of the subject in his December 1904 annual message, but indicated to reporters that he would submit a
special message on the tariff. He never sent the message. Instead,
he concentrated on obtaining legislation on the only matter he
had asked Congress to act on when he presented his 1904 annual
message, railroad rate regulation. That subject, incidentally, was
not even mentioned in the 1904 party platform. But it was politically safer than debate on the tariff, or trusts, or currency. The
outcome was the Hepburn Act, in early 1906, and no action on
the tariff whatsoever. Now and then, when faced with the political need to do so, he publicly stated that it appeared that it
would prove necessary to change the rates on some particular
items. Influenced by Senator Spooner, he also endorsed the idea
of having a tariff commission established to determine rate
changes, and he endorsed reciprocity.[6]

In a letter to Taft, while still Vice-president, Roosevelt summarized well his views on the tariff as a political issue. He wrote:

The protective tariff has vindicated itself in a most astonish-
ing way, . . . [but] when we admit that there should be any
change in the tariff the inevitable result is to strengthen those
who agitate for a disruption of the tariff. It is not easy to make
any change in the tariff policy without opening the door for all
sorts of changes. Personally I should think that the nation
would understand the need of continuity and steadiness of tar-

iff policy as far more important than all else. But when people are very prosperous they always think they can take liberties with their prosperity, and they never pay any heed to benefits that have accrued in the past as compared with any real or seeming trouble in the present.[7]

At least one historian, John Blum, has expressed belief that Roosevelt used the threat of tariff reform on leaders in Congress in order to force them into line on other matters.[8] I completely reject that interpretation. Neither logic nor the available facts support such a contention. To me, it is utterly fanciful to entertain such an idea. But he has succeeded in convincing many to accept his viewpoint.

Roosevelt's very limited performance on the important currency problem showed a lack of determination on his part to modernize the role of the government. Previous to the Panic of 1907, he demonstrated awareness of the woeful inadequacy of our currency and banking structure, but he shrank from taking positive action, even from asking Congress to create a commission to study the matter and make recommendations. In the wake of the 1903 financial crisis, some interested persons, including a few business leaders, had urged the commission approach.[9] One of these, Boston financier Henry L. Higginson, explained to the President that "the truth is, banking is well understood both here and abroad, and such a commission as you could appoint would give us a system that would last indefinitely. Such a system would be a great blessing and monument."[10]

Roosevelt, however, took the position that the commission approach was not feasible. In a letter to businessman John Byrne, he asserted that the Senate Four and Speaker of the House "Uncle Joe" Cannon represented such diverse interests that there could be no united Republican support in Congress for such a commission.[11] He explained to Byrne that,

Of course, the real difficulty comes from the fact that the different sections of the country seem to look at this question in different ways. If all the bankers and businessmen of New York

City felt alike, that of itself would be a stimulus to action by Congress; and if in addition the country bankers in districts like those in which Speaker Cannon lives felt the same way, we should be almost sure of legislation; but at present even the New York business world has but an indistinct idea of what it wants, and the country bankers of the Mississippi valley do not eye favorably what they have seen of the New York proposition.[12]

In his annual message to Congress, delivered December 7, 1903, Roosevelt showed something less than determined leadership when dealing with the problem. "The integrity of our currency," he said, "is beyond question, and under present conditions it would be unwise and unnecessary to attempt a reconstruction of our entire monetary system."[13]

On the problem of curbing the power of big business, Roosevelt showed more interest and spirit than in his dealing with the tariff and currency questions. Nevertheless, after a few initial steps, he backed away from inaugurating any genuine government control. He talked much about its need, but he proposed nothing concrete following the 1903 establishment of the Bureau of Corporations. He commendably supplied the initiative for the enactment of the Hepburn Act of 1906, regulating railroad rates, but that was a very limited advance in the light of the greater need for governmental control over big corporations. The problem was truly large and complex, and perhaps he could have made no more than a beginning, but one might wish Roosevelt had asserted himself more.

At the same time, we should remind ourselves that although less zealous in seeking economic reform legislation than he might have been, Roosevelt's goals for the relationship between business and government were not the same as those that prevailed in the world of big business. As Mr. Harbaugh said, "The corporate world wanted industrial stability and the maximization of profits. Roosevelt wanted the same things, but he wanted them because he deemed them crucial to the general welfare." Certainly, in contrast to the views of some of his friends, as

Mr. Harbaugh so aptly states, "The President's goal was a better, a more just and less privileged America; theirs, a more ordered America." In that connection, Mr. Harbaugh deserves some sort of special commendation. The item in his excellent essay that impressed me most was his discussion of the neo-Marxists' treatment of Roosevelt. It was well balanced, clearly delineated, true, and very useful.

Perhaps the best illustration of Roosevelt's awareness of business unreasonableness was his handling, in 1908, of the Hepburn bill, a measure not to be confused with the Hepburn railroad regulation act of 1906. The Hepburn bill of 1908 represented the culmination of the efforts of such powerful interests as the J. P. Morgan group and the influential National Civic Federation to obtain corporation immunity from prosecution under the Sherman Antitrust Act, accepting in its place a certain amount of governmental supervision. The measure was in keeping with Roosevelt's personal philosophy regarding the ideal relationship between government and business, but it clearly lacked adequate safeguards against possible business excesses. He refused to endorse it. The bill was buried in the House Committee on the Judiciary. But Roosevelt, incidentally, offered no alternative measure.[14]

I also agree with Mr. Harbaugh that Theodore Roosevelt's overall contribution to the future was substantial. As far as he went, he pointed the way to a stronger federal government and conducted himself in a highly moral manner. Because no taint of immorality, of corruption, or bad taste surrounded him or his associates, Roosevelt demonstrated that the profession of politics can be conducted on a high level of integrity and decency. With his example, we have a standard by which we can, if we choose, measure the quality of our public servants.

If, as Mr. Harbaugh believes, the time was not right for Roosevelt to do more, it must also be remembered that there was no Eleanor to needle his conscience at lunchtime. Instead, he had Henry Cabot Lodge and Elihu Root.

President Forever? Franklin D. Roosevelt and the Two-Term Tradition

Charles T. Morrissey

Richard nixon had his Camelot, too. It lasted briefly, from his sweeping victory over George McGovern in November 1972, to revelations of the Watergate scandals in 1973.

It is difficult now, knowing how Watergate reduced the Nixon presidency to shambles, to accept as plausible the talk in early 1973 that the 22nd Amendment to the Constitution (the two-term limitation on presidential tenure) should be repealed so Nixon could run for a third term in 1976. But ponder this historic relic from the *Wall Street Journal* of May 25, 1973:

> Watergate ripples fail to deter the mysterious Citizens for Nixon '76 from seeking repeal of the no-third-term amendment. The bipartisan group still plans to start a $4 million ad campaign in July. Richard DeLia, chairman of a New York ad agency aiding the drive, says "this has never been a wholly pro-Nixon group." He insists that the basic aim is simply freedom of choice.

Alas, we shall never know if Richard Nixon would have supported or tolerated an effort to repeal the 22nd Amendment, or if it would have succeeded. For him and his supporters it would have demanded a striking reversal of viewpoint. As a freshman member of the House of Representatives in 1947, Congressman Nixon voted for the proposed two-term limitation on presidential tenure. Every Republican in both houses of that famous 80th

Congress voted for it. Every state legislature which was controlled in both houses by Republicans between 1947 and 1951
also voted to ratify this proposed amendment. Republican
cohesion on this issue was remarkable in the state legislatures:
99.6 percent of the Republicans voting on it in 1947 voted for it,
and more than 96 percent voted for it during the four years it
was before the legislatures.

But Watergate has emphatically cast interest in repealing the
22nd Amendment into the dustbin of history. Without the
revelations about "dirty tricks" and all its consequences on the
Nixon presidency we would have watched to see if the 22nd
Amendment would have inhibited Nixon's power as his second
term moved along. Pundits had warned it would restrict President Dwight Eisenhower's power in Ike's second term; however those predictions about the 22nd Amendment causing
Eisenhower to become a "lame duck" after his 1956 victory were
wrong. "But in the latter part of his second term," Thomas A.
Bailey has written, "when he should have been quaking like a
crippled duck, he displayed more vigor and effectiveness than
at any other time during his incumbency." Bailey added:
"Evidently no one on his staff warned him that a lame duck is
supposed to waddle like one."[1]

And Spiro Agnew may recall, too, how some pundits predicted
the 22nd Amendment would bring strength to the Vice-president
as a party leader and help him win his party's presidential
campaign as the President's power receded due to the two-term
barrier.

Indeed, the history of the 22nd Amendment, since it was proposed in 1947, has many ironies. Congressman John Kennedy,
another freshman in the 80th Congress, also voted in favor of the
two-term limitation. He was one of only two Democrats in the
House from Northern urban districts so to vote (Representative
Edward J. Hart of Jersey City was the other), and this was a
discordant echo when Kennedy trumpeted the need for a strong
presidency in his 1960 campaign. If Kennedy had lived to run
against Barry Goldwater in 1964, and if he had won a victory as
overwhelming as Lyndon Johnson's, would JFK have obtained

FRANKLIN DELANO ROOSEVELT
January 30, 1882–April 12, 1945
The Thirty-second President of The United States

the support he desperately wanted to enact New Frontier legislation? Or would his mandate have ebbed away as rapidly as
Franklin Roosevelt's after the engulfing sweep of 1936?

And what of Lyndon Johnson, that zealous third-term supporter of Franklin D. Roosevelt in 1940, and still avid fourth-
term advocate in 1944, who forsook the second-term option
available to him by deciding not to run for reelection in 1968,
and afterward favored a single six-year term for Presidents?

We discuss today the question of presidential tenure—its
length and limitations—because many people worried that
Franklin Roosevelt wanted to be President forever. Their worries
sent the proposed 22nd Amendment through both houses of
Congress in 1947 (receiving more than the necessary two-thirds
support in each chamber) and through 24 Republican-controlled
legislatures by 1950. Let us not overlook the obvious in recalling
Franklin Roosevelt's impact on the office of the presidency and
the use of the power thereof: he was elected four times, twice as
many as any other candidate, and accordingly he served longer
than any other President. That length of tenure will never be exceeded unless the 22nd Amendment is repealed. Frankly, I doubt
that repeal will ever occur.

In a number of ways the 1940 victory for Roosevelt was crucial.
It aptly illustrates Louis Koenig's pithy phrase, "tenure is power."
For FDR it assured his own transition from "Dr. New Deal,"
trying to lead the nation out of the economic depression of the
1930s, to "Dr. Win-the-War" in the fight against the Axis nations.
For his supporters it meant that the New Deal was solidified and
isolationism rejected. For other Democrats who were denied a
chance for their party's nomination in 1940—James Farley especially—it meant a permanent setback to their aspirations. For
conservative Democrats, and Southern Democrats, it demonstrated the political power of a Northern-urban-labor-liberal orientation. For Republicans it meant not only their third defeat in
a row, but to some it was a link in a series of mistakes they long
afterward blamed on Roosevelt as the contriver of all their ills.
On the day the 22nd Amendment was ratified in 1951 a Repub-

lican congressman from Illinois, Noah Mason, summarized this viewpoint:

If this Amendment had been passed twenty years ago a sick President would not have gone to Yalta and surrendered to Stalin. We would not have spent 100 billions on a so-called Cold War. We would not be in Korea today and World War III would not be threatening. Instead of a 70 billion dollar tax load, our tax bill would be below 35 billion. There would be no need for federal controls, and best of all we would not now have Senator Harry Truman for President.

Reflecting upon a discussion with the President in 1937, Harold Ickes wrote in his diary that "the bough would be inclined as the twig had been bent in 1940." Roosevelt's critics as well as his defenders, when contemplating the third-term question in the late 1930s, could as easily have used the same words.

The passage of time causes us to overlook the emotional content of the third-term issue during FDR's second term, and the frustration his opponents experienced when a fourth term seemed likely. "A third term for Presidents is not something that normally excited positive enthusiasm, like booze or war," Henry L. Mencken wrote in the late 1930s; "it is something that excites only negative horror, like divorce, Wall Street, or smoking by women." Others stated their fears by conjuring all sorts of horrible imaginings if the two-term tradition were defied in 1940; Hugh Johnson warned that FDR might become a father to a line of kings: "A third term . . . and a fourth and a fifth term . . . a fifteenth term, and finally elect Jimmy Roosevelt and then start all over again."

To Alf Landon "the tradition against the perpetuation in office of the Chief Executive is as sacred as any the American boy learns at his mother's knee." He and other critics of the Roosevelt administration felt keenly that a third term would be alien to the American way of political life. Many of the people opposed to a third term summed up their feelings by saying "it's un-American." This fear was easily tapped: "It would undermine the democratic system more effectively than any subversive scheme the Reds themselves have devised and can hope to execute," warned the *Los Angeles Times.*

Other defenders of the tradition were convinced that it already had the legitimacy of a constitutional provision. "If the Constitution says nothing about a third term it also says nothing about the Supreme Court being exactly nine men, nor does it require electors to vote as pledged," argued Robert Bradford, a young Republican rising in Massachusetts politics. "A vote to end that tradition," he reasoned, "is as much a vote to change the basic theory of this republic as a striking out of those amendments to the Constitution which make up the Bill of Rights." Nicholas Murray Butler, president of Columbia University, maintained that the tradition had amended the Constitution in fact if not in form, and Samuel Pettingill, the former Indiana congressman, contended that it had been "silently ratified" by millions of Americans since 1787. The *Chicago Tribune*, despite its antipathy for everything British, pointed out that in England the unwritten tradition would have gained the stature of a constitutional provision. The absence of any words in the United States Constitution about a two-term limitation was cited by some of its defenders as further reason for honoring it. Irving Fisher, the Yale University economist, suggested in a letter to FDR that he not run in 1940 and offer the two-term tradition to justify his decision. "You can say, in effect, it is an unwritten part of our Constitution and one which, just because it is unwritten, should be especially cultivated and preserved, as something sacred, like the Ark of the Covenant."[2]

Their claims usually struck the President's supporters as ridiculous. The two-term precedent was "mere tradition" to William Gibbs McAdoo. To Rexford Tugwell it was "a sheer accident that no President in our history has yet had a third term." Harold Ickes said it was "political humbug." "As for your running for a third term," wrote a fervent supporter from Milwaukee, "I say GO TO IT! Two-term tradition—pooey! The greatest tradition is to right the wrongs and eliminate the causes that bring on all the wrongs."[3]

After listening to several Republican congressmen speak on the House floor about the inviolate nature of the two-term tradition, a Democratic member from California, Thomas F. Ford, expressed wonderment at their historical analysis.

They call upon high heaven to witness the admonitions of the founding fathers against a third term in spite of the fact that there is not one word in the Constitution that by the cunningest misreading or tenuous twisting could be made to appear as proscribing a third or any other number of terms for the President that the people happen to want.

Roosevelt's silence about his intentions in 1940 discomforted his supporters as often as it upset his opponents who feared he would challenge the two-term tradition. Representative Maury Maverick of Texas, a fervent supporter of FDR's most extreme legislative proposals, did not look forward to a third term in 1936: he sent a small statue of the "Saint of the Impossible" to the President for him to carry in his pocket when he departed the White House in 1941 after having accomplished several "impossible" feats during his second term. But Maverick was one of the first to urge a third term when a coalition of conservatives hobbled the New Deal in the second. "Mr. Roosevelt, stand by Franklin D. Roosevelt," was his advice to the President in 1939. "We Roosevelt people are anxious for Roosevelt to come out for Roosevelt and we hope he will be a good Roosevelt man." By February of 1940 Maverick's patience was turning into exasperation. When he invited the President to visit Texas to dedicate some federal projects he scribbled in ink across the bottom of his letter: "For Christ's sake—and this is said respectfully—go on and *RUN*."[4]

The public appetite for driblets of news and gossip about a possible third-term bid was voracious. Fred Rodell described it as "the most important, most discussed, most rumor-laden politi-

cal question in the United States today. . . ." "Bugs" Baer referred to the daily speculation as "the whether report"—whether
Roosevelt would run for a third term or whether he would not.
Walter Winchell played it safe by predicting at various times
that Roosevelt would run and would not run.

"The President continues to confuse us by saying absolutely
nothing on THAT subject," the *San Francisco Examiner* complained in March 1940. "It now looks as though the Third Term
will be the principal topic of conversation for everyone but
FDR until the Chicago convention." *The Saturday Evening Post*
ran a cartoon in which one gentleman, a Republican, lamented
to a colleague that Roosevelt might stay silent until it was too
late to hold the election. An insurance salesman in Kansas City
wrote to Roosevelt asking him to run again. "It's a tough job," he
admitted about the presidency, "but so is selling insurance." He
explained that "too many people that I call upon start discussing
the possibility of your candidacy for a third term—they won't
talk insurance but they will talk politics."5 Radio comedienne
Gracie Allen, with characteristic logic, offered a solution for the
entire problem: She said that Roosevelt should have run for the
third term first and then nobody would have objected when he
ran afterwards for the first and the second.

Roosevelt loved the mystery he had created by not revealing
his intentions, and his banter with the press became a regular exercise. Asked in the spring of 1939 whether he was going to run
again he replied: "Well, the answer is that this is 1939." Walter
Trohan of the *Chicago Tribune* asked about reports that he
planned to write newspaper columns—"Would that be 1940,
1944, or 1948?" Came the answer: "Oh, I could carry on both
jobs." In the laughter which greeted this remark he added,
"That will hold Walter." Asked what he thought about other
Democrats expressing their aspirations for the presidential nomination in 1940 he said he guessed the answer should be given by
"Number 57," but he declined to explain what he meant by
"Number 57."

His appointment of Paul McNutt in midsummer 1939 as head
of the Federal Security Administration was grist for the rumor

mills, but the President, when asked, said McNutt was only one of "a charming dozen young men" who could be considered for the nomination in 1940—and this caused the mills to grind more furiously. In August 1939, he was asked if he would like to say a few words about the 12th anniversary of an important event— Calvin Coolidge's "I do not choose to run for President in 1928." He joined the laughter and asked whether he was being invited to vacation in the Black Hills. Without waiting for an answer, he described his plans to cruise for a week in the North Atlantic.

Late in 1939, speaking at cornerstone-laying ceremonies at the Jefferson Memorial, the President looked up from his prepared text to say: "I hope that by January of 1941 I shall be able to come to the dedication of the memorial itself." This was interpreted by some to mean he wanted the memorial to be completed before his second term expired, and by others that he foresaw himself in the presidency even if completion was delayed until after January 1941. Shortly afterward at Hyde Park he admitted to newsmen that he had departed intentionally from his speech draft at the Jefferson Memorial in order to stir their curiosity about 1940.

"I watched the faces of everybody and they were funnier than a crutch," he howled. "And all of you fellows—oh, you have been having an awful time since." He could hardly control his satisfaction. "I did it deliberately and everybody bit." Two days later, dedicating the library building which would house his papers, he looked up from his text with a big smile to say: "And may I add, in order that my good friends of the press will have something to write about tomorrow, that I hope they will give due interpretation to the expression of my hope that when we open the building to the public it will be a fine day."

He said his family had accused him of taking an unholy pleasure in stirring up third-term speculation and he confessed that the charge was valid. But he did not curtail his fun. At the Gridiron Dinner during the Christmas season of 1939 a huge cartoon was displayed which pictured the President as a sphinx. FDR liked it so much that he obtained it and had it hung in his outer office at the White House, where it remained for several years. At the Jackson Day Dinner on January 14, 1940, he referred to himself with pleasure as a riddle.

To ask the President to declare his intentions, Walter Lippmann wrote, was "no more than a blunt demand that Mr. Roosevelt give himself up and confess." Lippmann realized that the President thrived on being mysterious and was skillful at it. "Mr. Roosevelt is too smart to leave fingerprints and tell-tale cigarette butts around . . . too tough to be bulldozed and too smart to be tricked."

Only a few times did Roosevelt become testy or tired of the persistent questioning. Afterward, when the reporters started probing again, the President usually gave the topic a humorous twist. Asked if he planned any statement for March 4, 1940, the seventh anniversary of his first inaugural, the President said he did not. "That will make Dave Lawrence mad," his questioner said about the anti-New Deal publisher of *U.S. News.* "Pass the tip to Dave that the first of April is good," the President chuckled.

When three newsmen told him in July 1940 that they had agreed to discuss the third-term issue on a radio program, the President wanted to know when the broadcast would begin. "11:15? My God, I will be asleep then." He suggested an earlier time. "If it were, perhaps, 9:15 or 9:45, I would give you something to say but I will be asleep, so what is the use?" On the same day he was reminded of what he had said back in February about declaring his political plans at a time of his own choosing. Would that time come before the convention? FDR rejected the question as "too iffy."

On the morning of the first day of the Democratic convention in Chicago a reporter put it to him bluntly: "Mr. President, I should like to ask you very honestly and sincerely why you have refrained from making your position known on the third-term question?" The President replied by saying Senator Alben Barkley would make an announcement to the convention that evening. "But your answer to my question did not answer my question," the newsman protested. Roosevelt smiled: "Of course it did not."

Barkley's message to the Democratic convention that evening, in essence, was contained in two sentences: "The President has never had, and has not today, any desire or purpose to continue in the office of President, to be a candidate for that office, or to be nominated by the Convention for that office. He wishes in all earnestness and sincerity to make it clear that all the delegates to this Convention are free to vote for any candidate."

What did this mean? A goodly number probably appraised it as Eleanor Roosevelt did as she heard it on the radio at Hyde Park. It did not say yes or no about his candidacy, she later told the President on the telephone, but by not saying no it did, in effect, say yes. Predictably, the convention gave FDR the draft he wanted.

After he decided to seek a third term, a large number of President-watchers offered retrospective judgments as to when he had made the decision. Many are sure that the decision was definite and final, even if they disagree as to when it occurred. Harry Bates, a student who looked into the subject closely, has written that, "The third term decision will probably be the best guarded political secret of the twentieth century for many years."[6]

For many of Roosevelt's critics there was nothing secretive or uncertain in the President's behavior in 1939 and 1940; the plot had been clear to them long beforehand. John Shafer, a Republican congressman from Wisconsin, asserted that the third term was part of a plan conceived on November 16, 1933, when the United States extended diplomatic recognition to Soviet Russia. Raymond Moley thinks the third-term candidacy was "fore-ordained" in the same year. "One morning [in 1933], after Lewis Douglas, then Budget Director, had completed his early morning conference in the Roosevelt bedroom and had left, I said something in his praise. Roosevelt agreed and then added thoughtfully, 'In twelve years he would be a good Democratic candidate for President.'" This remark, Moley has claimed, "indicated a purpose in his mind, even at that early date, to break tradition and to try for a third term."

Others believe the decision was entwined with what they perceive as the salient characteristic of Roosevelt's personality, his drive for power, and argue that his victories in 1932 and 1936 simply made him hunger for more. Thus they date it with repeal of the "two-thirds rule" in the 1936 Democratic convention, or the "Court-packing" of 1937, or the "purge" of 1938. Those who believe that Roosevelt deliberately involved the United States in World War II cite the delivery of the "Quarantine Speech" in 1937 as the time of decision. Some do not date it, because they feel it was always his intention: "In the 'sticks' we have known for several years that FDR is working for dictator powers of [the] United States," a constituent wrote to Senator William E. Borah.[7] Jesse Jones was convinced that Roosevelt would die with the harness on his back: "In my view, when he found what he could do with the radio, he made up his mind to stay President as long as he lived, if possible, and to take such course from time to time as seemed most likely to achieve this object."[8]

People to whom the President confided his intention to quit after two terms were not always convinced. Arthur Krock was granted a special interview with the President in February 1937, and Roosevelt told Krock he wanted to retire to Hyde Park in 1941. Krock came away from the interview convinced that Roosevelt would run again, regardless of a statement to the contrary. The fact that Roosevelt permitted the interview, irrespective of what was said, was sufficient evidence for Krock that the President was contemplating a third term and trying to disarm those who might not be sympathetic toward it. "I could see no other reason for it," he has insisted.[9]

A good proportion of the President's strongest political supporters was similarly skeptical of his willingness to relinquish the top spot. Sam Rayburn in 1961 met a young man in his twenties who was introduced as a graduate student trying to ascertain when Roosevelt decided to seek a third term. "That shouldn't be so hard to figure out," the Speaker said curtly. And one longtime assistant to the President, who worked closely with him in the White House and developed a deep admiration for him, was firmly convinced that "they'd never get him out of the White House unless they carried him out in a box."[10]

For the most part, however, his ardent supporters believed that the third-term decision was made late in the game and was due to Roosevelt's sincere belief that continuity of presidential leadership was required because of the danger posed by war abroad. Samuel Rosenman and Edward Flynn, for example, date the decision at May or June 1940, after France had fallen to the Nazis. Paul Appleby believed that Roosevelt did not finally make up his mind until all the pieces were in place, and this he dates as the day after the convention had nominated him for the presidency and had accepted FDR's choice of Henry Wallace as the vice-presidential candidate.

Historians who probe the "secret" and try to pinpoint a time of decision probably come no closer than Roosevelt's contemporaries, most of whom in their writings and remembrances reveal more of their own attitudes toward Roosevelt than Roosevelt's attitude toward a third term. Reading the diaries, memoirs, and other personal accounts of the Roosevelt era is "a game of You Pays Your Money and Takes Your Choice," as Jerome Frank has put it. Each chronicler was free to interpret the bits of evidence revealed to him in accordance with his own hopes and fears.

Rarely did a man confess his perplexity as frankly as David Lilienthal did to his diary after a session with the President: "But if anyone could tell from the expression on his face or from those words what was in his mind about running again, or could make out any answer to the enigma from his remarks about a reactionary successor, he is a better reader of signs than I am; . . . he has certainly done a masterful job in keeping his own counsel on the most important single question the country has today: Will he be the next President?"

To select a particular day or span of days as the time when Roosevelt decided to seek a third term on the basis of who indicated what to whom is risky, because Roosevelt, the complete politician, often told his listeners what he figured they wanted to hear. And he was constantly reassessing his own judgments and revising them accordingly. "Of course, I think it is useless to speculate on what the President is going to do about a successor," Ickes wrote in his diary in September 1938. "He may be thinking of Harry Hopkins today and about someone else tomorrow, trying to feel his way to a wise, definite conclusion."

His operating style, moreover, was a shield against those trying to penetrate his thinking. Ickes once blurted out what many of Roosevelt's intimates felt: "You are a wonderful person but you are one of the most difficult men to work with that I have ever known."

"Because I get too hard at times?" the President asked.

"No," Ickes replied, "you never get too hard but you won't talk frankly even with people who are loyal to you and of whose loyalty you are fully convinced. You keep your cards close up against your belly. You never put them on the table." Roosevelt admitted that the indictment was justified, but he never changed his ways. "Once the opportunity for decision came safely into his orbit," Arthur M. Schlesinger, Jr., has written, "the actual process of deciding was involved and inscrutable."

Tugwell has developed this point even further, arguing that Roosevelt tried to camouflage his decisions by creating the appearance that no choosing had taken place. "It is no accident," Tugwell has pointed out, "that it is impossible to find in all of the Roosevelt papers, or even in the memoirs of his intimates, leads to the functioning of his deciding apparatus. He became so skillful in concealing his deficiencies, and his hurts because of them, that he could never find it possible to reveal his inner self to anyone—and neither his mother nor his wife was an exception to this." Tugwell claims that it is possible to understand why Roosevelt made certain important decisions, but not possible to explain how they were made. "The how will never be fully known. There may be glimpses here and there as notes and memoirs of associates come to light, but Roosevelt himself never made any—even if he understood the processes of his own mind, as few of us do, and the mechanisms are unlikely ever to stand clearly revealed."

Donald Richberg has written similarly about the problem of probing the "inner Roosevelt."

During several years I had many opportunities to observe

FDR closely, while working with him both in the stress of crowded days and in the comparative calm of long evenings, while lunching with him at his desk on the terrace outside his office, swimming in the pool at the White House or Warm Springs, or travelling with him by train, or on the Presidential yacht. This apparent intimacy might seem to provide ample basis for at least a partial understanding of the inner man whose purposes, ambitions and prejudices motivated the actions of the outer man who occupied what became in Roosevelt's time the most powerful public office in the world. But I would be the last to claim that I ever became well acquainted with the inner man.

Roosevelt knew that his array of alternatives would retract if he committed himself to men and viewpoints while issues were evolving. He tended to view the future as a variety of possibilities which would develop from a set of current probabilities. "Roosevelt's plans were never thoroughly thought out," Frances Perkins maintained. "They were burgeoning plans; they were next steps; they were something to do next week or next year. One plan grew out of another." His style reminded her of an artist "who begins his picture without a clear idea of what he intends to paint or how it shall be laid out upon the canvas, but begins anyhow, and then, as he paints, his plan evolves out of the material he is painting."

His political education had provided ample opportunities for learning the value of procrastination. He knew that decisions could be postponed until the time to make them was clear and the choice was obvious, or until issues had subsided so action was unnecessary. As governor of New York, Frances Perkins recalled, he had delayed continually in taking action against a particular person until the patience of his friends was exhausted. "And then," Miss Perkins added, "the man died!"

Roosevelt hated the "irrevocability of decision," to use John Gunther's phrase, and guarded carefully against the possible intrusion of an unexpected element that might upset a decision. Watching Roosevelt in the presidency reminded his loyal sup-

porter, Senator Joseph Guffey of Pennsylvania, of an occasion
when the two men were scheduled to participate together in a
public ceremony and Roosevelt asked Guffey to check the lectern beforehand to see if it could support the weight he would
put on it. "The incident of the lectern came often to my mind
during the Roosevelt years," Guffey has written, "for it was
typical of an innate caution in the man, something few realized
because it was so overshadowed by the drama of his stagecraft.
Behind the spectacular display of cool daring that left his
supporters breathless and his enemies in fury, there was the
man who always checked his stage props before the curtain rose,
leaving to chance and fortune only those things which could
not be anticipated or predicted. He made sure that the platform
would 'support his weight' before he took any irrevocable
step."[11]

Thus Roosevelt knew he did not have to take that final step
toward a third-term candidacy until the time arrived when he
could no longer be silent about his intentions. The occasion for a
public announcement could be deferred until the Democratic
convention was actually underway. Of equal benefit, by that
time he could assess a wide range of contingencies, especially the
war abroad and its implications for America. He sensed that he
could not safely challenge the two-term tradition unless the urgency of the international situation were to justify this departure
from political custom. By waiting until midsummer 1940, he
could also obtain a last-minute judgment of domestic conditions
at home, and political realities such as who would run if he did
not and who would head the party if he did not.

The future was full of forebodings: aggressive nations in Europe and Asia might threaten the United States, which seemed
somnolent about its security; the New Deal might be undone;
the party might relapse into conservatism; the Republicans
might win. To seek a third term, and lose, would jeopardize too
much. The fury of oratory which the Republicans would unleash
about his defiance of the two-term tradition, if he did seek reelection, would surely be immense. By waiting upon events he
knew that circumstances would indicate whether he could de-

flect those charges of vaulting ambition in winning a third term. Time provided him with what he needed: When Americans gasped with horror at the power of the Nazi juggernaut moving across Europe, the President knew he could confidently risk a third bid.

During the 1940 campaign the sacredness of the two-term tradition was holy doctrine for loyal Republicans. In their platform they pledged to work for a Constitutional Amendment limiting the President to no more than two terms in office, and Wendell Willkie promised this would be his first item of business after being inaugurated. In every one of his 550 speeches he referred to FDR as "the third-term candidate," and the issue was the one to which Republicans were most responsive. When Willkie challenged the President, in his 1940 campaign kickoff speech in Elwood, Indiana, to debate the third-term issue, the crowd cheered wildly for several minutes. Later, in Los Angeles, when he concluded a speech by declaring, "We don't have to have a third term," the reaction was an avalanche of cheering.

Indeed, it is possible that Republicans who were uncertain about Willkie as their candidate (he was, after all, liberal in attitude toward many domestic problems, and an interventionist until the last three weeks of the campaign), compensated for their doubts by emphasizing Roosevelt's disdain of the two-term tradition. "Almost without exception," the *New Republic* observed of the Republican wheelhorses, "they paid lipservice to their tousle-headed boy and shouted against the third term." Late in the campaign Richard Neuberger noticed in the Western states that Republicans explained they would vote for the GOP not because they liked Willkie but because they disliked Roosevelt, and they were replacing their Willkie buttons with "No Third Term" buttons.

The Democrats tried to ignore the third-term issue. One study of the 1940 campaign has estimated that fully 85 percent of all references to the third-term issue were expressions by opponents of it. When the Speaker of the House of Representatives in the Philippine Islands arrived in Washington in early October 1940 to obtain the President's signature on a new constitution for the Philippines, he reported first to Harold Ickes, because the Department of the Interior then had jurisdiction over the Islands. Ickes leafed through the new constitution and was startled to see that it contained a two-term limitation on the president of the Philippines. "Listen, Bud," Ickes told the distinguished envoy from the Philippines, "you go up to the Mayflower and get yourself a nice comfortable room and wait until *after* the November election before you ask FDR to sign anything like that." The gentleman did exactly what he was told.

During Roosevelt's third term his supporters could chuckle easily at the discomfort of their Republican rivals. Parents were telling their children, according to one anecdote which made the rounds, that if they were ambitious and hard-working they might grow up to become *Vice*-president. Bob Hope, the comedian, remarked at a Washington banquet in the spring of 1944, just before Wendell Willkie entered (and lost) the crucial Wisconsin primary, that "Willkie has his eye on the presidential chair, but look what Roosevelt has on it." Senator R. Owen Brewster of Maine, traveling in North Africa on a military inspection trip in 1943, looked wistfully at the Pyramids and the Sphinx and commented, "As a Republican, you know, I'm reassured to note that even the great Egyptian dynasties came to an end." His colleague, New Deal Senator James Mead of New York, did not object to Brewster's assumption that the Democratic ascendancy would terminate eventually. "Even as a Democrat," he responded, "I'll gladly settle for a term like that one—it ran for over a couple of centuries."

Roosevelt certainly did not underplay his role as Commander-in-Chief during his third term in the presidency. "Will you permit me to urge you to run for reelection?" Governor Herbert Maw of Utah asked him in a letter written in July 1943. The President delayed a response to Maw's query for several months: "Its arrival found me engaged with our Chiefs of Staff, preparing for the Quebec Conference," he explained. "I must ask you to believe me when I tell you that my one consideration now is to win this war. It is a stern and difficult business. My responsibility is great and I feel that I would not be keeping faith with the trust which the people have given me and in my legal responsibilities as Commander-in-Chief of our armed forces if I were to give any consideration whatsoever to my Presidential election which is more than a year away."[12]

When he publicly announced his willingness to serve a fourth term he reversed General William Tecumseh Sherman's famous disclaimer about not accepting the nomination if offered and not serving if elected. "If the Convention should nominate me for the Presidency," he asserted, "I shall accept. If the people elect me, I shall serve." To Robert Hannegan, chairman of the Democratic National Committee, he wrote: "If the people command me to continue in this office and in this war, I have as little right to withdraw as the soldier has to leave his post in the line." His nomination for a fourth term seemed so ordained that Helen Gahagan Douglas described FDR as the "Forgotten Man" of the 1944 Democratic convention. And many felt that the election itself was assured from the outset. "It seems to me that the fourth term, like the first, was inevitable," William Hassett wrote in his diary. "That leaves the second and the third to be accounted for by the Roosevelt haters."

The President enjoyed the predicament facing his opponents. He repeated to visitors a remark Elmer Davis had made about the war: "Some people want the United States to win so long as England loses. Some people want the United States to win so long as Russia loses, and some people want the United States to win so long as Roosevelt loses."

The Republican platform repeated the 1940 pledge to initiate a constitutional limitation of two terms on the presidency, and Thomas Dewey as the party's nominee promised to support this pledge if elected. Dewey fumed about 1940: "At that time Mr. Roosevelt represented himself as indispensable to America. Now, four years later, he seeks a fourth term upon the claim that he is indispensable to the world."

Hard-core Republicans responded enthusiastically to such rhetoric. They cheered when Clare Booth Luce itemized the alleged mistakes of an administration "elected again and again and again." "Yes," Mrs. Luce declared, "history will certainly relate the story of the Seventy Eighth Congress [elected in 1942] as a long and bitter struggle by the legislative branch of the Government to wrest from the executive branch the proper restoration of those powers which, if there had been no third term, would naturally have returned to it." Senator Edwin Johnson of Colorado, a conservative Democrat and New Deal critic, looked back at 1940 in the same way: "The greatest tragedy of American political history was the President's decision four years ago to seek a third term." He characterized the third term as "the term of appeasement" because Democrats were willing to accept the President's dominance of their party. "The Democratic Party is no longer democratic. One man will name its candidate for President, its candidate for Vice-President; and write its platform, just as was done in 1940. If it materializes, history will name the fourth term the term of frustration."

A fourth term would entail "four more years of WPA all over the world at the expense of the American taxpayer," Senator Styles Bridges of New Hampshire warned, and "four more years of using the White House powers to build a national Tammany Hall." In one speech the Republican Senator pointed out that, "There are people in this audience who since Mr. Roosevelt first was elected have come of age, married, had children, watched their children grow up to go to school, and faced this question at the dinnertable, 'Daddy, has Mr. Roosevelt always been President?' I have a son in the armed forces of this country in foreign service. He is old enough to fight for his country, yet he cannot remember any President but Roosevelt." In response to such lamentations, Governor Matthew Neely of West Virginia warned of "crepe on 10,000,000 doors" if FDR was not allowed to prosecute the war until the enemy was defeated.

When Joseph Guffey argued on the Senate floor that Republicans should not object to a fourth term because the issue of tenure had been settled by Roosevelt's third-term victory in 1940, a newspaper reporter visualized the Republicans as muttering to themselves, "Yes, damn it, that was just what we argued in 1940, to no avail."

Roosevelt having won a fourth term in 1944, it seemed to some of his opponents that the long night of their discontent would never find a day. At a press conference on the day before the fourth inaugural, the President quipped that "the first twelve years were the hardest," and Mae Craig perked up at this. "I am wondering, Mr. President, about the significance of the word *first?*" Everybody laughed. A moment later another reporter asked: "Is this the last four years?" The President laughed and said, "Jim, you're just as bad as the rest." At sea on the trip to the Yalta Conference the President's birthday was celebrated with five birthday cakes—one for each term and a fifth with a question mark drawn in the frosting.

Roosevelt carried 38 of the 48 states in his campaign against Wendell Willkie in 1940, and in 1944 he carried 36 states against 12 for Governor Thomas Dewey. In the Electoral College, the margin for Roosevelt was 449 to 82 in 1940, and 432 to 99 in 1944. These figures suggest that both victories were won decisively. Similarly, historians and others who have tried to estimate the number of votes Roosevelt lost because of his defiance of the two-term issue in 1940 have concluded that the loss was minor.

William Langer and S. Everett Gleason, for example, have suggested that Roosevelt probably attracted enough votes from Republican interventionists to offset the number he lost to conservative Democrats who were unhappy about the third term and the New Dealism of the party. Samuel Lubell has estimated that whatever the third-term issue cost Roosevelt was compensated for by the number of new voters in 1940 who chose to support him.

Louis Bean, in his book, *How to Predict Elections*, figured that the Democrats should have picked up 30 seats in the House of Representatives instead of seven in 1940, and that the difference was due to the reduced size of Roosevelt's coattails because of the third-term issue. Since 62 percent of all the Democratic candidates for the House were successful, Bean argues, Roosevelt's percentage of the two-party total vote should have been 57.5 percent, not 55 percent. "Therefore, it may be estimated that the third-term issue cost Roosevelt a maximum of about 2.5 percent of nearly fifty million votes, or, allowing for a margin of doubt in our formula, 1 to 1.5 million." A post-election survey conducted by Paul Lazarsfeld and two other social scientists concluded that the no-third-term argument served as a "real" converting force for only about 2 percent of the total Republican vote, and this estimate of 2 percent they felt was generous. The *New Republic's* post-election guesswork in 1940 produced a comparable figure. Because Roosevelt received 1,116,000 less votes in 1940 than he did in 1936, "you might say if you like that the difference between this year's vote and the figure reached by adding his previous total to the normal Democratic percentage of the natural growth of the population probably represents the number of people frightened off by the third-term issue."

Hardly a Republican failed to specify the third term when asked to explain why he voted for Willkie. But, asking people to explain why they voted as they did, as experts on voting behavior have pointed out, is rarely an adequate means for getting to the basis of their choices. "Many people who had voted for Roosevelt in 1936 said they were against a third term," Warren Moscow has written of his observations in the state of New York in 1940.

Many millions of words were written and spoken that year about the importance of the "third-term issue." In every case I encountered, by pressing for more than casual information, I found that the voter disapproved of a majority of acts in the previous four years, making it highly probable that not one of the persons interviewed would have voted for Roosevelt in 1940 had he been running then for only a second term. Possibly some few persons in the state and nation in 1940 really preferred Roosevelt to Willkie and nevertheless voted for Willkie on the third-term issue, but I did not meet any. I did meet hundreds who used the third-term candidacy as a conversational short cut in explaining their switch.

But these analyses overlooked the extent to which Roosevelt's third-term victory was due to "an upsurging of the urban masses," as Lubell phrased it.[13] Urban America was strong for the third term; rural America was not. Every city in the nation of more than 500,000 population voted for Roosevelt, and 91 of the 95 cities of more than 100,000 population voted for him, too. Outside the urban North and West and outside the old Confederate states the President trailed Wendell Willkie by 600,000 votes. For example, Willkie carried rural and small-town Ohio by 94,000 votes, but lost Ohio to Roosevelt because FDR carried its industrial centers. Willkie led Roosevelt by 127,000 votes in downstate Illinois but Chicago's huge Democratic plurality won the state for FDR. In these and other states, when the proposed two-term limitation was submitted for ratification in the rural and small-town-dominated state legislatures, the anti-Roosevelt voters of 1940 and 1944 had their revenge. Bear in mind that ratification was achieved in 1951, before the Supreme Court ruled in the case of *Baker* v. *Carr* for reapportionment of state legislatures in states where urban residents were underrepresented. The representation of these cities in the state legislatures, based on an estimate in 1938, averaged only three-fourths of what it should have been if representation had been equitable. This imbalance increased during and after World War II until the average city resident of the early 1950s had approximately one-half the representation in about 36 state legislatures that his country cousin had.

Several state legislatures had been inundated only briefly by the New Deal tides that swept many Democrats into office in 1932, 1934, and 1936. For three decades the Republicans in Michigan had controlled every session of the state legislature; they lost control in the 1930s for only a single session and then regained it for another quarter century. Some states like Minnesota and California had voted Democratic from 1932 to 1948 in national elections but had been strongly Republican on the state level since 1938. The GOP controlled both houses of 24 legislatures as a result of the 1944 election, and added another in 1946.

After the two-term tradition was broken, moreover, many

anti-Roosevelt voters looked back to 1940 as the crucial turning-point in recent history. Time did not heal the wounds suffered in that dark hour. "He had to re-elect himself in 1940," Senator Arthur Vandenburg wrote in 1944, "and in order to do so he *had* to say in Boston on the eve of the 1940 election, 'I have said this before, but I shall say it again and again and again: your boys are not going to be sent into any foreign war.' . . ."

Some who had voted for Roosevelt soon after had qualms about their decision. "I immediately regretted having voted for a third term," John Dos Passos later recalled. "That inaugurated the 'Caesar style' in American politics: spend, spend, spend; tax, tax, tax; elect, elect, elect."

Many felt as Representative Joseph Martin did—that the third term was not emphasized sufficiently by the Republicans in the 1940 campaign. One anti-Roosevelt historian, Eugene E. Robinson of Stanford University, has written that protests against the third nomination "were mild indeed compared with what might well have been said about the significance of such action."

The frustration of the anti-New Dealers was assuaged slightly when Harry Truman began his tenure as Roosevelt's successor. "During the three months that Mr. Truman has been in the White House the country has gotten what it has long wanted but could not get," Walter Lippmann wrote in the summer of 1945. "The country has wanted a new administration; but it could not take a Republican administration dominated by the Taft-Martin wing of the Republican party." On the other hand, Lippmann figured, "the country did not want a third and a fourth term," so Truman fit the country's mood.

But advocates of tenure limitation did not waver. "A vigorous effort is being made to restore Congress to its old position of influence in our Government," Joe Martin announced in the summer of 1945. "The first step in this program to restore popular government in America should be the submission by Congress to the several states of a Constitutional Amendment to limit the tenure of office of a President to two terms of four years each."[14]

But this appeal did not stir a noticeable response. Not until the Truman honeymoon ended and the troubles of post-war adjustment and the Republican cry of "Had Enough?" heralded a GOP landslide in the 1946 elections, did the time become appropriate for this step. Republicans were as jubilant in November 1946 as New Deal Democrats had been ten years before. Both Houses of the 80th Congress would be controlled by Republicans for the first time since Herbert Hoover was President. One observer of the hearty handshaking and bold talk about fulfilling campaign promises among GOP members of the concluding 79th Congress compared the scene to the excitement on a small college campus after its football team had upset the national powerhouse from the state university.

This feeling had not diminished when the 80th Congress assembled. After electing Joe Martin as Speaker of the House seven Republicans introduced proposals to limit by Constitutional Amendment the tenure of the President to no more than two terms. Passage of this legislation was the first major accomplishment of the 80th Congress.

Republican enthusiasm for ratifying the proposed two-term amendment did not slacken because the chances for a Republican President seemed so promising in 1948. To the contrary, in the spring of 1948 a poll of 3500 Republican party-workers in New York State disclosed that ratification of this proposal was third in the number of issues they considered to be of principal concern at that time. Control of labor unions and the reduction of government spending were given top priority, then ratification of this amendment. Behind ratification came the housing shortage, high prices, and all issues in foreign policy. In the heat of the campaign in October the Republican vice-presidential candidate, Governor Earl Warren of California, urged an audience in Columbus, Ohio, to vote Republican in November to assure ratification of the two-term amendment.

Understandably, when various state legislatures convened in early 1951, the stage was set for increasing from 24 to the necessary 36 the list of states which had already ratified. Five states which had not ratified—Indiana, Idaho, Wyoming, Montana, and Utah—had elected Republican majorities in both houses in November 1950. In five more states—Minnesota, Maryland, South

Carolina, Alabama, and New Mexico—where one house of the legislature had previously ratified, the mood was growing to urge the other house to vote approval. This mood in early 1951 included a variety of complaints against the accumulated policies of the Roosevelt-Truman era—from opposition to Truman's civil rights program among white Southerners to discontent nationally with what the Republicans encapsulated and ballyhooed in the 1952 campaign as "Korea, Communism, and Corruption." Democratic-controlled legislatures joined the Republicans in ratifying the two-term amendment. Nevada, the 36th and decisive state, ratified on February 28, 1951; the final number of states which ratified grew to 41 of the 48.

Franklin Roosevelt's defiance of the two-term tradition, and the subsequent passage of the 22nd Amendment, is a curious chapter in this nation's long and continuing history of dealing with presidential power. In effect, the 22nd Amendment stands as a monument to Franklin Roosevelt's unique success in winning four electoral victories. Undoubtedly his critics did not intend to memorialize his achievement in this way. It is an ironic outcome of their belief that presidential power could be restrained if tenure could be limited, by constitutional dictum, to two terms.

It will be ironic, also, if the 22nd Amendment proves in the future to be a liberating tool for some second-term President who wants to use his power wisely. But it will be tragic if it allows a President to abuse power because he knows in his second term that he can avoid being responsive to the electorate. The recent history of the two-term issue, consequently, provides us with an uncertain legacy.

The Impact of
Franklin D. Roosevelt's Four Terms

Donald R. McCoy

THE POLLING of historians on the relative greatness of Presidents is one of Clio's most popular parlor games. It is also one of the least rewarding. Few scholars, if any, know enough about all of the Presidents so that they can make such fine distinctions as to rank Grover Cleveland, for example, eighth, tenth, or fourteenth, as he has been in various polls. After all, Presidents operate within a specific segment of time and their records are considerably governed by the then-existing conditions and public attitudes. They can exploit conditions and manipulate attitudes, but they can rarely create them. Moreover, the criteria for assessing Presidents change from time to time, reflecting the shift in ideas and interests in each new wave of historians.

It is better that historians eschew intellectual parlor games and instead devote themselves to dealing with the available facts. Their job is to consider what happened at a given time and in a given place, to reconstruct, analyze, and interpret the evidence in so far as they can. In short, the overriding question for a historian of a presidency is: How did the President respond to the challenges and opportunities of his time and with what impact? If a President is to be compared with other Presidents, it can, in fairness, be only on the basis of impact, and with due consideration for the fact that some Presidents have had more opportunity for impact and for a reputation for greatness than have others.

With regard to Franklin D. Roosevelt, there can be no doubt

159

that he had great impact on the United States, perhaps more than any other President. This is attributable partly to his extraordinary length of service, partly to the fact that his administration had two monumental crises to which to respond, and partly to the nature of that response.

Unusually self-confident, the squire of Hyde Park sparkled with ideas and optimism. He was the supreme pragmatist, committed both to the survival of basic American ideals and to his own personal success. Thanks to the coming, first, of depression and, then, of world war, Roosevelt was the man on the spot, but he made it clear that he could accommodate the ferocious tides of his time. He made it equally plain who was chief. A man who had vanquished a crippling disease, he was willing to try anything within reason and sometimes things beyond reason. He also believed that he could usually tame anything and anybody. Sensitive to the wants of the majority, and above all charmingly articulate, he was a master at dealing with his subordinates and with the people.

His receptiveness to innovation and dramatic action was foreshadowed in 1932 when he broke tradition and flew to Chicago to accept the Democratic presidential nomination in person. Roosevelt's 1933 Inaugural Address, given at the depth of economic depression, sounded the keynote for his administration. His call then for "action, and action now" can well be considered the motto for most of his more than 12 years in the White House, and it had the approval of a large majority of Americans.

Quickly emerging after Roosevelt's inauguration was the program that has been labeled the Three R's—Relief, Reform, and Recovery. Of these, the Roosevelt administration's greatest success was in the area of relief to the needy. Utilizing new and multiple approaches and agencies, the New Deal provided subsistence living to most of America's huge number of unemployed. The administration's reforms were unprecedented in number and far-reaching in effect. Banking, the stock market, public utilities, trade unions, agriculture, natural resources, blacks, Indians, housing, the aged, the handicapped, and the government itself were among those significantly touched by federal reforms. Of course, the New Deal's reforms were sometimes contradictory and often far from adequate. They nevertheless represented the greatest amount of reform achieved by government action in the United States. Far less successful, however, were the administration's efforts to achieve economic recovery for the nation. About three-quarters of those unemployed in 1933 were still out of work in 1939, and as many Americans were receiving some form of government relief in 1939 as in 1933. When prosperity finally returned, it was borne on the shield of Mars instead of on the serving trays of the New Deal. In all fairness, though, the administration must be given some credit for taking advantage of World War II to spread prosperity around.

Yet, all this was far from being the sum of the Roosevelt administration's impact. Roosevelt masterfully exploited his political opportunities to construct a new majority political coalition. Successfully appealing to racial, religious, and ethnic minorities, labor, city dwellers, intellectuals, and even some farmers and small businessmen, Roosevelt was able to change the political party affiliation of the majority of Americans from Republican to Democratic. One result was that the Democrats were to win seven of the ten presidential elections and 18 of the 20 congressional elections between 1932 and 1970. At least equally important, this reflects the fact that Roosevelt and his associates sold the American people on big government as the guarantor of economic and military security. The Roosevelt administration also encouraged secrecy in government—especially during World War II—and laid the basis for the rise of what is called the government-military-industrial complex.

Another result of the administration was the great change in the nature of federalism and the separation of powers. Americans more frequently looked to Washington instead of to the state capital for action, and states found themselves involved in a wide range of joint programs in which the federal government imposed the objectives and standards. Within the national government, the executive branch became the segment that usually initiated as well as implemented federal programs, as Congress not only increased the responsibilities but also the power of the executive sector. By 1940, the states seemed to be largely clients of Washington, and Congress appeared to be chiefly a body to modify or veto executive action.

What all this meant was that the Roosevelt administration greatly reinterpreted the role of the federal government. Not only did Washington intervene in the economy, but it espoused the objective of providing satisfaction for almost everybody, which presaged greater intervention later on. And this was not just at home, for America's wartime aims included no less than reforming the world in the democratic image of the United States. That goal was carried across to the post-war world, even if it meant the continuation of a high level of military preparation, the rearing of a vast international intelligence organization, and the fashioning of a great program of economic reconstruction. Whatever one thinks of all this—and it decidedly has both merits and demerits—one cannot deny its tremendous impact on both the United States and the rest of the world.

This leads directly into the burden of Charles Morrissey's essay. The 22nd Amendment is a fact of political life in the United States. It will probably continue to be so indefinitely, given its rather precise provisions and the almost complete lack of success of past movements to repeal amendments to the Constitution. Considering the amount of space available here to discuss our topics, we have had to be selective. Mr. Morrissey decided to limit his essay to one single aspect of the impact of the presidency of Franklin D. Roosevelt. He chose well, in that the election of Roosevelt as President beyond two terms is a significant part of the New Yorker's impact and one which is seldom properly considered today. In effect, it has had double-edged consequences. One, it extended the tenure of this remarkable presidency beyond the traditional maximum of eight years and, two, it led to a limiting reaction which raises important and ongoing questions for Americans.

In the first case, the extra years that Roosevelt had in office gave his administration time to extend its impact as well as to cement many of its earlier actions. This is clearly seen in the continuation and even acceleration of many economic regulations and regulatory agencies, as well as of the ideas of executive branch primacy, high taxation, the welfare state, and the domination of the federal government over the states. It is also witnessed in the greater control by the White House over executive agencies, additional opportunities for the lower economic classes and minority groups, the rise of the military, internal security, and governmental secrecy, and the great change in American public opinion toward involvement abroad. In other words, most Americans by 1945 were conditioned to support big, pervasive, paternalistic, internationalist government.

Harry S. Truman, regardless of the problems facing him, carried on in the Roosevelt tradition during both his first term, which he owed to inheriting the remainder of the New Yorker's last term, and his second term as President. It is doubtful that Thomas E. Dewey, had he been elected to the White House in 1948, would have significantly altered the state structure existing at that time, because of the popular acceptance of big government. Certainly, the Presidents since Truman have not. I am not suggesting that, had someone else, say James Farley or Wendell Willkie, been chosen President in 1940, the result would necessarily have been substantially different. It might have been, however, and a change would have been more easily accomplished without the extra years in the White House of Roosevelt and the additional reinforcing years of Truman.

In the second case, Roosevelt's decision to stand for a third term as President forced the American people to give serious consideration to restricting the Chief Executive constitutionally to two terms. Of course, that only began then. Roosevelt lost votes in 1940, to be sure, but there were, after all, a number of other questions that contributed to his reduced margin of victory, whether they be the trivial "I Want to be a Captain Too" issue or the far more important questions of America's defense preparations and its stance vis-à-vis war in Europe. This is not to say that Roosevelt's decision to seek a third term was a small issue in 1940. It was, however, definitely one that most American voters were unprepared to contest. Franklin Roosevelt was too strong a political figure and held too deep a place in the affections of a majority of the people. In 1940, and even in 1944, they trusted him as they would trust no other politician.

The third-term issue could, however, be brought up effectively during the Truman administration. Harry Truman at no time commanded the confidence and affection that Roosevelt had. Moreover, President Truman's civil rights, international, and economic policies alienated a sizable number of Americans. Many of them also had second thoughts about Roosevelt during the late 1940s, partly because some of the newly prosperous wanted less government intervention and partly because others held Roosevelt responsible for the postwar foreign-policy dilemmas of the United States. Then, too, Truman was not as adept as Roosevelt had been in attracting popular and legislative support. Republicans and anti-administration Democrats therefore had no trouble in shepherding through Congress the 22nd Amendment and in gaining its ratification by the state legislatures. In short, the third-term ban was imposed both as a form of revenge against the departed Roosevelt (and what he represented) and as a rebuke to Truman, who, though legally exempted from the 22nd Amendment's provisions, could hardly successfully go against the amendment's spirit.

There were, no doubt, Americans who supported the 22nd Amendment solely on its philosophical merits, without reference to Roosevelt and Truman, but they probably constituted a very small minority. Yet, no one who supported the amendment could ignore the theoretical arguments in its favor. There was a lot of quoting of Lord Acton's famous observation that "power tends to corrupt; absolute power corrupts absolutely." More important was the view that the people should have the frequent opportunity to change their government, relatively uninhibited by the personality and power of the incumbent.

It is doubtful that the presidency has been weakened by the 22nd Amendment. Dwight D. Eisenhower was, if anything, more innovative and successful during his second term than during his first, and Senator George S. McGovern did not indicate that he thought a second term for President Nixon would have any less impact than his first term. As for Franklin Roosevelt, his second term was less effective than his first, but it is unlikely that that was significantly because his opponents thought it would be his last term. It is clear that, under the circumstances of 1937–1940, it would have been difficult for any President to have equaled the impact of Roosevelt's first term. The support for "action, and action now" was overwhelming then, and the mistakes and the ebbing vitality of the New Yorker during his second term were equally clear. The idea that a second and supposedly last term robbed Roosevelt of effectiveness was largely a convenient excuse for the administration's apologists and for unimaginative analysts of events.

I want to close my commentary with a few quibbles and questions and a dissent. The decisiveness of Roosevelt's 1940 election victory cannot be measured precisely just in terms of the electoral vote and the number of states won. Neither accurately reflects the popular vote, which is the gauge of citizen sentiment. Indeed, one can theoretically carry a majority of the states and still not win the majority of either popular or electoral votes. The ballots cast by individual citizens in 1940 represented a more considerable change in Roosevelt's popularity than is suggested by Mr. Morrissey. The President attracted 445,000 fewer votes in 1940 than in 1936, and, more important, Wendell Willkie polled 5,647,000 more votes than Alfred M. Landon had four years earlier. This accounted for a significant drop in Roosevelt's margin of victory between 1936 and 1940— from slightly more than 11,000,000 votes to less than 5,000,000 and from 62.5 percent of the popular vote cast for major-party presidential nominees to 55 percent. And Roosevelt was on his way to only 53 percent in 1944, compared to 47 percent for Thomas Dewey, which was hardly a runaway win. Another statistical problem is that one cannot talk, in trying to assess the impact of the third-term issue on Roosevelt's 1940 campaign, about the Democrats winning seven seats in the House of Representatives and yet ignore the fact that the Republicans picked up five seats in the United States Senate. The point of all this is that statistical analysis is a defective tool when essential data go unrecognized.

Furthermore, one cannot simply say that "Roosevelt's third-term victory was due to 'an upsurging of the urban masses.' " This applies even if—or maybe especially if—one's source is Samuel Lubell. After all, Roosevelt had carried the vast majority of cities in 1936. If he expanded his urban support in 1940, it was probably attributable to the militant support of labor unions, the membership of which had skyrocketed since 1936 from 3,989,000 to 8,717,000. Yes, Roosevelt's third presidential election was vitally based on city votes, but that had been true of his second and, though to a lesser extent, first victories.

Regarding the ratification of the 22nd Amendment, it is open to debate whether urban underrepresentation in the state legislatures made any substantial difference. Most of the states that ratified were not dotted by big cities anyway, and the majorities among legislators voting in other states were often so heavy that it is questionable whether equal representation, had it existed then, would have prevented the ratification of the 22nd Amendment. The difference, in favor of the amendment, might have been made by the population shift after the war to the suburbs, which were inclining toward conservative voting patterns. Roosevelt's fourth-term victory could also have made the difference, for it strengthened sentiment for restricting Presidents to a maximum of two terms. After all, the fourth term did make Roosevelt "President forever," whether or not that was his aim.

As for the question of whether the 22nd Amendment has strengthened the position of the Vice-president in American politics, not enough time has elapsed really to tell. Although Richard M. Nixon, in 1960, and Hubert H. Humphrey, in 1968, failed in their bids for the presidency, it must be kept in mind that they were strong enough to gain presidential nominations and to run close contests. Their failures at the polls could be considered personal, not institutional or constitutional. Moreover, there is the fascinating question of whether Nixon could have come back from political oblivion to win the presidency in 1968 if it had not been for his vice-presidential background, experience, and contacts. The overall question of the relationship between the political strength of the Vice-president and the 22nd Amendment, of course, requires far more detailed analysis, for factors other than the amendment have to be considered.

I shall end on a note of dissent. Mr. Morrissey indicates in his paper that he believes the success of a President is the prime reason for assessing the impact of the 22nd Amendment. I strongly disagree with that, for a President's success can run counter to the best interests of the people, and indeed sometimes has proved at least the first part of Acton's axiom. The merit of the 22nd Amendment can be assessed only in terms of how it has benefited the people and how it has reinforced the effectiveness of constitutional politics and government. I see no evidence that it has harmed society, government, or politics in the United States. Indeed, I would suggest that it has benefited them by keeping American politics fluid as well as by working against the development of an entrenched national political machine. This, I submit, is a positive benefit in a democratic republic, for no single leader, whether a Roosevelt from New York or an Eisenhower from Kansas, is indispensable among free, educated men and women.

APPENDIX

Appendix: The Schlesinger Polls on Presidential Greatness

How DO historians rank American Presidents? Which ones were great, near great, average, below the average, or outright failures?

These were the questions asked by Arthur M. Schlesinger, Sr. in 1948 and again in 1962. The first survey included 55 experts—professional historians, political scientists, and journalists—and the second was expanded to include 75 views, including most of the original 55 pollees. An attempt was made to provide a geographical cross section, and the opinions of three Britishers were also sought.

The survey listed all Presidents who had served an appreciable time, including in the 1962 poll Dwight D. Eisenhower, a recent incumbent. The only exclusions were William H. Harrison and James A. Garfield, who had served less than a full year. The sole test of greatness was performance in office, and the participants were instructed to disregard anything the President accomplished before or after serving in office.

Here are the results of the two polls:*

---

*The complete text of the 1948 polls, with Schlesinger's interpretation of the results, can be found in Arthur M. Schlesinger, Sr., *Paths to the President* (New York: Macmillan, 1949). The 1964 *Sentry* edition of the same volume, published by Houghton Mifflin in Boston, contains the results of the 1962 poll, with Schlesinger's comments on the changes since 1948.

THE SCHLESINGER POLLS

1948 Poll	*1962 Poll*

GREAT

1. Abraham Lincoln	1. Abraham Lincoln
2. George Washington	2. George Washington
3. Franklin D. Roosevelt	3. Franklin D. Roosevelt
4. Woodrow Wilson	4. Woodrow Wilson
5. Thomas Jefferson	5. Thomas Jefferson
6. Andrew Jackson	

NEAR GREAT

7. Theodore Roosevelt	6. Andrew Jackson
8. Grover Cleveland	7. Theodore Roosevelt
9. John Adams	8. James K. Polk
10. James K. Polk	9. Harry S. Truman
	10. John Adams
	11. Grover Cleveland

AVERAGE

11. John Quincy Adams	12. James Madison
12. James Monroe	13. John Quincy Adams
13. Rutherford B. Hayes	14. Rutherford B. Hayes
14. James Madison	15. William McKinley
15. Martin Van Buren	16. William Howard Taft
16. William Howard Taft	17. Martin Van Buren
17. Chester A. Arthur	18. James Monroe
18. William McKinley	19. Herbert Hoover
19. Andrew Johnson	20. Benjamin Harrison
20. Herbert Hoover	21. Chester A. Arthur
21. Benjamin Harrison	22. Dwight D. Eisenhower
	23. Andrew Johnson

BELOW AVERAGE

22. John Tyler	24. Zachary Taylor
23. Calvin Coolidge	25. John Tyler
24. Millard Fillmore	26. Millard Fillmore
25. Zachary Taylor	27. Calvin Coolidge
26. James Buchanan	28. Franklin Pierce
27. Franklin Pierce	29. James Buchanan

FAILURE

28. Ulysses S. Grant	30. Ulysses S. Grant
29. Warren G. Harding	31. Warren G. Harding

NOTES

NOTES

Louis W. Koenig (Pages 1–15)

1. O. E. Tiffany, "The Relations of the United States to the Canadian Rebellion of 1837–1838," *Buffalo Historical Society Publications* 8 (1905), 33–35.
2. See, for example, James Reston, *The Artillery of the Press* (New York, Harper and Row, 1967), pp. 45–47; and Arthur Schlesinger, Jr., "Presidential War," *New York Times Magazine*, January 7, 1973.
3. William L. Langer and S. Everett Gleason, *The Undeclared War* (New York: Harper and Brothers, 1953), *passim*.
4. See Tom Wicker, "Making War, Not Love," *New York Times*, January 14, 1973.
5. Bernard Gwertzman, "Report to Nixon Cites Concern on Johnson's Decision-Making," *New York Times*, January 12, 1969.
6. James Reston, "Thunder on the Right," *New York Times*, January 19, 1973.
7. Louis W. Koenig, *The Chief Executive* (New York, Harcourt, Brace and World, rev. ed., 1968), pp. 214–215.
8. For background on anti-Vietnam war amendments and the war powers bill, see *Guide to Current American Government* (Washington: Congressional Quarterly, 1972), pp. 89–93.
9. C. M. Thomas, *American Neutrality in 1793: A Study in Cabinet Government* (New York: Columbia University Press, 1931).
10. *U. S. Foreign Policy for the 1970s: A New Strategy for Peace; A Report to the Congress by Richard Nixon, President of the United States, February 18, 1970* (Washington, D. C.: U. S. Government Printing Office, 1970), pp. 17–23.
11. Alexander M. George, "The Case for Multiple Advocacy in Making Foreign Policy," *American Political Science Review* LXVI (September 1972), 751–791.
12. Theodore C. Sorenson, *Kennedy* (New York: Harper and Row, 1965), pp. 679–680, 684–686.
13. George, *op. cit.*, 784–785.
14. Thomas A. Johnson, "New Power of Welfare Clients," *New York Times*, August 7, 1971.

Edward Pessen (Pages 16–25)

1. In an article on how 55 scholars in 1948 ranked American Presidents, Arthur M. Schlesinger, Sr., reported that Van Buren was rated 15th among 29 Presidents judged, in the middle of the "average" category that came below the ten "greats" and "near greats," and above the eight Presidents evaluated as "below average" or "failures" (*Life*, 25 [November 1, 1948], 65ff). By 1962 Van Buren's standing dropped

slightly as Schlesinger's authorities now placed him 17th among the 31 Presidents ranked (*The New York Times,* July 29, 1962). Nor has Van Buren's reputation among scholars improved in the past decade. In a more detailed questionnaire than either of Schlesinger's, that was answered by 571 of 1095 randomly selected members of the Organization of American Historians, Van Buren comes off as "above average" only in "flexibility"—a trait contemporaries would have equated with insincerity and lack of principle. Van Buren was placed near the bottom third of Presidents for general prestige, strength of action, presidential decisiveness, idealism, and in the accomplishments of his administration (Gary M. Maranell, "The Evaluation of Presidents: An Extension of the Schlesinger Polls," *Journal of American History,* LVII [June, 1970], 104–113).

2. Edward Shepard, *Martin Van Buren* (New York, 1899); Denis Tilden Lynch, *Epoch and a Man: Martin Van Buren and His Times,* 2 vols. (Port Washington, 1929); and Holmes Alexander, *The American Talleyrand: The Career and Contemporaries of Martin Van Buren* (New York, 1935).

3. John C. Fitzpatrick, ed., "The Autobiography of Martin Van Buren" (American Historical Association, *Annual Report,* Washington, D. C., 1920). Van Buren begins his account, written at Villa Falangola, in Sorrento, June 21, 1854, as follows: "At the age of 71, and in a foreign land, I commence a sketch of the principal events of my life" (*Autobiography,* p. 7.) Professor Ferree is in the midst of what he advises me is a most laborious process of checking the accuracy of Van Buren's recollections.

4. Shepard, *Martin Van Buren,* p. 400.

5. *Autobiography of Martin Van Buren,* p. 226.

6. *Ibid.,* p. 168.

7. *Ibid.*

8. Edward Pessen, *Jacksonian America: Society, Personality, and Politics* (Homewood, Illinois, 1969).

9. Interestingly, each of these Presidents is ranked much higher than Van Buren by modern historians. Polk, once known as "the mendacious," is apparently ranked "near great" because of his role in leading the nation into a war that resulted ultimately in a great expansion of its territory, despite a widespread belief that he was less than candid in explaining the incidents that led to this war and misgivings concerning the underlying motives of his war policy.

10. McCormick comment on my paper on Van Buren, September 15, 1972, at the Tarrytown Conference on Six Empire State Presidents. When Mr. McCormick speaks, sensible men listen. See his magisterial *The Second American Party System: Party Formation in the Jacksonian Era* (Chapel Hill, N. C., 1966).

11. Letter to the author, April 20, 1972. I await Mr. Cole's biography with interest, but I must note that nothing in John K. Mahon's authoritative *History of the Second Seminole War 1835–1842* (Gainesville, Fla.,

1967), suggests that Van Buren, whatever his private doubts, took significant public actions to deflect the course of that dubious war.

12. James C. Curtis, *The Fox at Bay: Martin Van Buren and the Presidency, 1837–1841* (Lexington, Ky., 1970).

13. Pessen, *Jacksonian America,* p. 190.

14. Curtis, *The Fox at Bay,* p. 63.

15. Edward Pessen, "The Egalitarian Myth and the American Social Reality: Wealth, Mobility, and Equality in the 'Era of the Common Man,'" *American Historical Review,* 76 (October, 1971), 989–1034; George Blackburn and Sherman L. Richards, Jr., "A Demographic History of the West: Manistee County, Michigan, 1860," *Journal of American History,* LVII (1970) 613, 618; and Gavin Wright, "'Economic Democracy' and the Concentration of Agricultural Wealth in the Cotton South, 1850–1860," *Agricultural History,* 44 (1970), 63–94.

16. Bray Hammond, *Banks and Politics in America from the Revolution to the Civil War* (Princeton, N. J., 1957), p. 496.

17. "Autobiography" of Martin Van Buren, p. 394.

18. E. Merton Coulter, ed., *The Other Half of Old New Orleans, Sketches of Characters and Incidents from the Recorder's Court of New Orleans in the 1840's as Reported in The "Picayune"* (Baton Rouge, La., 1939), p. 73.

19. Marvin Meyers, *The Jacksonian Persuasion* (Stanford, Calif., 1957), p. 149.

20. Robert V. Remini, *Martin Van Buren and the Making of the Democratic Party* (New York, 1959).

Robert J. Rayback (Pages 33–50)

1. Until the publication of Robert J. Rayback's *Millard Fillmore, Biography of a President,* Buffalo: 1959, the literature on Fillmore, except for articles in biographical encyclopedias and passing reference in general works such as DeAlva S. Alexander, *Political History of the State of New York,* 4 vols., New York: 1906, was confined to two 1856 campaign biographies (W. L. Barre, *The Life and Public Services of Millard Fillmore,* Buffalo: 1856, and [Ivory Chamberlain] *Biography of Fillmore,* Buffalo: 1856) and a first effort to mine the newly discovered (1907) Fillmore manuscripts by Frank H. Severance in his introduction as editor to *Millard Fillmore Papers,* 2 vols., Buffalo Historical Society, *Publications,* 10, 11, Buffalo: 1907, followed by William F. Griffis' *Millard Fillmore,* Ithaca: 1915, a short and unanalytical account inspired by the manuscripts.

2. Weed, Harriet A., ed., *Life of Thurlow Weed including his Autobiography and a Memoir,* 2 vols., Boston: 1883–4, I, 584–88; Van Deusen, Glyndon G., *Thurlow Weed, Wizard of the Lobby,* Boston: 1947, opposite p. 150.

3. "Fillmore's Autobiography of His Earlier Years," in Severance, *Fillmore Papers,* II, 3–15.

4. Severance, Frank H., ed., *The Picture Book of Earlier Buffalo*, (Buffalo Historical Society, *Publications*, 16) *passim;* Lord, John C., "Samuel Wilkeson," *ibid.*, vol. 4, pp. 11–85; Poole, Martha F., "Social Life of Buffalo in the '30's and '40's," *ibid.*, vol. 8, pp. 443–7; Larned, J. N., *A History of Buffalo*, 2 vols., Buffalo: 1911, I, 137–43; Rapp, Marvin, *Rise of the Port of Buffalo*, Chapel Hill, N. C., pp. 28ff.

5. See Robert G. Albion's classic *Rise of the Port of New York, 1815–1860*, New York: 1939, for the port's growth, and Ira Rosenwaike, *Population History of New York City*, Syracuse: 1973, ch. 3.

6. A full discussion of Fillmore's activities as lawyer and public official before he became President can be found in Rayback, *Fillmore*, chs. 3, 5, 7, and 9.

7. Joseph Story to Fillmore, Nov. 12, 1851. Fillmore Collection at the Buffalo Historical Society contains the original clippings and manuscripts of Fillmore's speeches on this New England tour. Severance edited them to a considerable degree before he put them in *Fillmore Papers*, II, 482ff.

8. The story of American involvement in the Orient is told in many places with varying degrees of detail and emphasis. For its treatment as a continuing action in American politics before the Civil War see Leonard Pudelka, "The Whig Party's Far Eastern Foreign Policy, A prelude to Imperialism," doctoral dissertation, 1972, Syracuse University. Fillmore's role is set forth more completely in Rayback, *Fillmore*, pp. 293–317.

9. Webster, Daniel, *Writings and Speeches of Daniel Webster*, National Edition, 18 vols., Boston: 1903, vol. 16, 322.

10. For the general story of Anti-Masonry's origin in New York, see Hammond, Jabez D., *History of the Political Parties of the State of New York*, 3 vols., Syracuse: 1852, II, 287ff.; Van Deusen, *Weed*, chs. 3 and 4; McCarthy, Charles, *The Anti-masonic Party: A Study of Political Antimasonry in the United States, 1827–1840* (*Annual Report of the American Historical Association*, 1902), Washington, 1903. For Fillmore's role, see Rayback, *Fillmore*, ch. 2.

11. *Ibid.*, ch. 5.

12. Nowhere did Fillmore, or any other contemporary, set forth these lessons as guidelines. They are the author's extrapolations as he tried to establish a base to give the tangled, contradictory politics of Fillmore's day a matrix of consistency, logic, and reality.

13. For an overview of the Compromise, see Hamilton, Holman, *The Compromise of 1850*, Indianapolis, 1963, and *Zachary Taylor*, 2 vols., Indianapolis, 1941–1951, vol. 2.

14. Oran Follett, a Whig soothsayer and well-wisher, a former editor of the *Buffalo Journal* and supporter of Fillmore, gave the phrase currency through his Sandusky, Ohio, *Journal*. See clippings in Oran Follett Papers, Ohio Archaeological Society, Columbus, for 1844–45. Eventually, Follett's "new departure" became "Conscience Whiggery," but the flavor of the words "new departure" indicates the practical purpose of the Whigs' new "conscience."

15. An early academician who recognized the plight of Southern Whigs and the drive of the "Young Indians" to promote Taylor as a means of resolving the problem was George Poage in his *Henry Clay and the Whig Party*, Chapel Hill, 1936, pp. 152–196.
16. See Rayback, *Fillmore*, pp. 192–206.
17. Armond, George D., "Douglas and the Compromise of 1850," *Journal of the Illinois Historical Society*, Vol. 21, 451–99.
18. Hamilton, *Taylor*, vol. 2, 377, 378.
19. Rayback, *Fillmore*, pp. 239–53.
20. *Ibid.*, chs. 14 and 15.
21. After Fillmore retired from the presidency, he retained and acted on his belief that political polarization along geographical lines would invite secession. As a way of avoiding that catastrophe, Fillmore permitted himself to be used as the focus to deepen political alliances on a national basis. His candidacy for the American Party in 1856 represented a supreme personal sacrifice to attain that end. Nativism, as tribal prejudice, was only an adhesive for the American Party's more realistic goal.

Charles M. Snyder (Pages 51–58)

1. Robert J. Rayback, *Millard Fillmore, Biography of a President,* Publications of the Buffalo Historical Society, vol. 40 (Buffalo, N. Y., 1959).
2. Fillmore's personal papers, supposedly burned in conformity with the will of his son, were discovered at New Haven, N. Y., in 1969. They are now at the State University of New York, Oswego. See *New York Times*, Apr. 28, 1969, and Charles M. Snyder, "Forgotten Fillmore Papers Examined: Sources for Reinterpretation of a Little Known President," *The American Archivist*, vol. 32, 11–14.
3. Harriet Prewett to Millard Fillmore, Sept. 25, 1857. Fillmore Papers, State University of New York, Oswego.
4. Millard Fillmore, *Millard Fillmore Papers*, ed. Frank H. Severance, 2 vols., Publications of the Buffalo Historical Society (Buffalo, 1907), 2, 86.
5. Albert D. Kirwin, *John J. Crittenden: The Struggle for the Union* (Lexington, University of Kentucky Press, 1962), p. 264.
6. Holman Hamilton, *Prologue to Conflicts the Crisis and Compromise of 1850* (Lexington, University of Kentucky Press, 1964), pp. 184–187.

Thomas C. Reeves (Pages 59–74)

1. "The Tragedy in The Depot," *New York Times*, July 3, 1881.
2. "The Week," *The Nation*, XXXIII (1881), 1.
3. Editorial, "To Whom It May Concern," *New York Times*, July 3, 1881.
4. Actually, the public was informed that Arthur was born in 1830. For the complex story of the switch in dates, see Thomas C. Reeves, "The Mystery of Chester Alan Arthur's Birthplace," *Vermont History*, XXXVIII (1970), 291–304.

5. See "General Arthur Dead," *New York Commercial Advertiser,* November 18, 1886; Chauncey M. Depew, *My Memories of Eighty Years* (New York, 1922), p. 117.

6. Claude M. Fuess, *Carl Schurz Reformer* (New York, 1932), pp. 272–273.

7. "The Week," *The Nation,* XXXI (1880), 445. On the details of Arthur's nomination, see "Garfield and Arthur," *New York Times,* June 9, 1880; *New York World* dispatch of June 10 in "More of Gov. Dennison's Foolishness," *Cleveland Leader,* June 21, 1880; William Henry Smith to Rutherford B. Hayes, June 15, 1880, in Charles Richard Williams (ed.), *Diary and Letters of Rutherford Birchard Hayes* (Columbus, Ohio, 1924), III, 605; "Gath," *Cincinnati Enquirer,* August 14, 1883; William C. Hudson, *Random Recollections of An Old Political Reporter* (New York, 1911), pp. 96–99; Robert McElroy, *Levi Parsons Morton, Banker, Diplomat and Statesman* (New York, 1930), pp. 105–106; Chauncey M. Depew to A. B. Samford, June 3, 1920, Chauncey M. Depew Papers, Yale University.

8. Editorial, *New York Times,* November 3, 1880.

9. Editorial, *Chicago Evening Journal,* April 8, 1881.

10. See Albert B. Paine, *Thomas Nast: His Period and His Pictures* (New York, 1904), 449, 486–487.

11. "A Talk With Gov. Foster," *New York Times,* July 3, 1881.

12. Editorial, "President Arthur," *ibid.,* September 21, 1881.

13. George F. Hoar, *Autobiography of Seventy Years* (New York, 1903), II 46.

14. Julia Sand to Arthur, September 28, 1881, Chester A. Arthur Papers, Library of Congress.

15. John S. Goff, "President Arthur's Domestic Legislative Program," *New-York Historical Society Quarterly,* XLIV (1960), 167.

16. Harriet S. Blaine Beale (ed.), *Letters of Mrs. James G. Blaine* (New York, 1908), II, 4–5.

17. H. J. Eckenrode, *Rutherford B. Hayes: Statesman of Reunion* (New York, 1930), p. 335.

18. Louis J. Lang (ed.), *The Autobiography Of Thomas Collier Platt* (New York, 1910), p. 182.

19. "Arthur's Popularity," [Washington] *Commercial Advertiser,* November 19, 1886.

20. Brodie Herndon diaries, entry of August 1, 1882, Brodie Herndon Papers, University of Virginia.

21. "Gath," *Cincinnati Enquirer,* in Chester A. Arthur Scrapbooks, Columbia University, II, 150.

22. Brodie Herndon diaries, entry of May 23, 1882, Brodie Herndon Papers, University of Virginia.

23. See E. J. Edwards, "New News of Yesterday," a 1911 clipping in the Charles Pinkerton Collection, currently in the author's possession. The literature on Arthur's declining health is rather large. See especially: "Arthur's Health," *Indianapolis Journal,* October 9, 1882; "President Arthur's Health," *New York Herald,* October 21, 1882; "President Arthur

in Town," *New York World*, January 23, 1883; Chester A. Arthur to Chester A. Arthur II, March 11, 1883, Chester A. Arthur II Papers, Library of Congress; "Dead Among His Kindred," *New York Times*, November 19, 1886; "General Arthur Dead," *New York Commercial Advertiser*, November 18, 1886; "Twice Critically Ill," *Philadelphia Times*, December 10, 1886; "Chester A. Arthur Dead," *New York Sun*, November 19, 1886.

24. See notes of the interview between Frank B. Conger and Vernon B. Hampton, September 9, 1933, Vernon B. Hampton Papers, in Mr. Hampton's possession, Staten Island, New York. See also notes of the interview with Arthur H. Masten, November 25, 1931. Arthur also asked his Secretary of the Navy, William E. Chandler, not to attend the convention. "Anecdotes of Mr. Arthur," *New York Sun*, November 28, 1886. He refused to permit Cabinet members to be active on his behalf in any way. See Elmer Ellis, *Henry Moore Teller, Defender of the West* (Caldwell, Idaho, 1941), p. 158. He even discouraged Stalwart boss John A. Logan from lending assistance. See Margarita Spalding Gerry (ed.), *Through Five Administrations: Reminiscences of Colonel William H. Crook* (New York, 1900), p. 280.

25. Robert D. Marcus, *Grand Old Party: Political Structure in the Gilded Age 1880–1896* (New York, 1971), p. 76.

26. Alexander K. McClure, *Recollections of Half A Century* (Salem, Mass., 1902), p. 115.

27. William E. Chandler, "Chester A. Arthur," in James Grant Wilson (ed.), *The Presidents of the United States 1789–1914* (New York, 1914), III, 235.

28. "Arthur Statue Unveiled," *New York Sun*, June 14, 1899.

Kenneth E. Davison (Pages 75–83)

1. *New York Herald Tribune Books*, November 11, 1934.

2. The most recent of these articles, published since the Tarrytown Conference, is: Thomas C. Reeves, "The Search for the Chester Alan Arthur Papers," *Wisconsin Magazine of History*, Vol. 55, No. 4 (Summer, 1972), 310–319.

3. H. Wayne Morgan, *From Hayes to McKinley: National Party Politics, 1877–1896* (Syracuse: Syracuse University Press, 1969), p. 148n.

4. Kenneth E. Davison, *The Presidency of Rutherford B. Hayes* (Westport, Conn.: Greenwood Press, 1972), pp. 81–85.

5. See for example: Thomas C. Donaldson, "Memoirs," December 9, 1880, pp. 144–147, typescript copy in Rutherford B. Hayes Library, Fremont, Ohio (RBHL).

6. Hayes Diary, August 9, 1885; Hayes to Fanny Hayes, November 19, 1886; Hayes Diary, November 21, 1886, all in RBHL.

7. Hayes deliberately inserted a self-denying proclamation of his "inflexible purpose" to serve for only a single term in his Letter of Acceptance of July 8, 1876.

8. Wilfred E. Binkley, *The Man in the White House: His Powers and Duties*, Revised edition (New York: Harper & Row, 1964), p. 240.
9. Donaldson, "Memoirs," January 30, 1880, p. 126.

Vincent P. DeSantis (Pages 84–100)

1. Samuel Eliot Morison, Henry Steele Commager, and William E. Leuchtenburg, *The Growth of the American Republic*, 2 vols, 6th ed. (New York: Oxford University Press, 1969), II, 162.
2. Allan Nevins, *Grover Cleveland, A Study in Courage* (New York: Dodd, Mead and Company, 1933), p. 766.
3. Morison, Commager, and Leuchtenburg, *Growth of the American Republic*, II, 162.
4. Nevins, *Cleveland*, p. 5.
5. Richard Hofstadter, *The American Political Tradition and the Men Who Made It* (New York: Vintage Books, 1959), p. 180.
6. Thomas A. Bailey, *Presidential Greatness, The Image and the Man from George Washington to the Present* (New York: Appleton-Century-Crofts, 1966), p. 29.
7. Gary M. Maranell, "The Evaluation of Presidents: An Extension of the Schlesinger Polls." *Journal of American History*, LVII (1970), 104–113.
8. Henry Adams, *The Education of Henry Adams* (New York: Modern Library, 1931), pp. 294, 355.
9. James Bryce, *The American Commonwealth*, 2 vols. (New York and London: Macmillan and Co.), II, 29.
10. Morison, Commager, and Leuchtenburg, *Growth of the American Republic*, II, 162.
11. Quoted in Leonard D. White, *The Republican Era, 1869–1901* (New York: Macmillan Co., 1958), 21, 24, 41.
12. Allan Nevins, ed., *Letters of Grover Cleveland, 1850–1908* (Boston and New York) Houghton Mifflin Company, 1933), p. XI.
13. James D. Richardson, *A Compilation of the Messages and Papers of the Presidents 1789–1897*, 10 vols. (Washington, D. C.: Published by Authority of Congress, 1899), VIII, 774.
14. Rexford G. Tugwell, *The Enlargement of the Presidency* (Garden City, New York: Doubleday and Co., 1960), p. 247.
15. Richardson, *Messages and Papers of the Presidents*, VIII, 557; IX, 390.
16. Bailey, *Presidential Greatness*, p. 224.
17. Louis W. Koenig, *The Chief Executive* (New York: Harcourt, Brace and World, 1964), p. 11; Horace Samuel Merrill, *Bourbon Leader: Grover Cleveland and the Democratic Party* (Boston: Little, Brown and Co., 1957), p. 190; Tugwell, *Enlargement of the Presidency*, p. 250.
18. Nevins, *Cleveland*, p. 766.
19. Morison, Commager, and Leuchtenburg, *Growth of the American Republic*, II, 162.
20. Richardson, *Messages and Papers of the Presidents*, VIII, 302.

21. Quoted in Marcus Cunliffe, *American Presidents and the Presidency* (London: Eyre and Spottiswoode, 1969), p. 179.
22. Quoted in Vincent P. De Santis, "Grover Cleveland," in Morton Borden, ed., *America's Eleven Greatest Presidents*, 2nd. ed. (Chicago: Rand McNally, 1971), pp. 166–167.
23. White, *Republican Era*, p. 25.
24. Quoted in Cunliffe, *American Presidents*, p. 145.
25. Sydney Hyman, "What is the President's True Role," *New York Times Magazine*, September 7, 1958, pp. 17ff.
26. Tugwell, *Enlargement of the Presidency*, p. 248.
27. James Morgan, *Our Presidents* (New York: Macmillan Co., 1935), p. 221.
28. William Allen White, "Cleveland," *McClure's Magazine*, 18 (1901–1902), 325.
29. Joel Benton, "Retrospective Glimpses of Cleveland," *Forum* 40 (1908, 193.
30. Wilfred E. Binkley, *That Man in the White House, His Powers and Duties*, rev. ed. (New York: Harper Colophon, 1964), p. 56.
31. Henry L. Stoddard, *As I Knew Them* (New York: Harper and Brothers, 1927), p. 153.
32. Nevins, *Cleveland*, p. 640; Tugwell, *Enlargement of the Presidency*, p. 238.
33. Bailey, *Presidential Greatness*, pp. 41–42; Tugwell, *Enlargement of the Presidency*, p. 476.
34. Tugwell, *Enlargement of the Presidency*, p. 313; Cunliffe, *American Presidents*, p. 185.
35. Bailey, *Presidential Greatness*, p. 300.
36. Hofstadter, *American Political Tradition*, p. 185.

William H. Harbaugh (Pages 107–124)

1. Howard K. Beale, *Theodore Roosevelt and the Rise of America to World Power* (New York, Collier ed., 1966), p. 387, *passim*.
2. William Henry Harbaugh, *Power and Responsibility: The Life and Times of Theodore Roosevelt* (New York, Farrar, Straus & Cudahy, 1961), p. 522.
3. *The Life and Times of Theodore Roosevelt* (New York, Collier ed., 1963), and William H. Harbaugh (ed.), *The Writings of Theodore Roosevelt* (Indianapolis, Bobbs-Merrill, 1967).
4. *The Writings*, p. xiii.
5. *The Life and Times of Theodore Roosevelt*, pp. 288–89.
6. *The Writings*, pp. xxvi–xxvii.
7. *Ibid.*, xxxiii; *Power and Responsibility*, p. 339; *The Life and Times of Theodore Roosevelt*, p. 321.
8. *Power and Responsibility*, p. 327.
9. Quoted in the Washington *Post*, January 28, 1973.
10. Gabriel Kolko, *The Triumph of Conservatism* (Glencoe, Ill., The Free Press, 1963).

11. Samuel P. Hays, *The Response to Industrialism, 1895–1914* (Chicago, University of Chicago, 1957); Robert H. Wiebe, *The Search for Order: 1877–1920* (New York, Hill & Wang, 1968); James Weinstein, *The Corporate Ideal in the Liberal State* (Boston, Beacon Press, 1968).

12. *Power and Responsibility.* pp. 229–230.

13. Arthur M. Johnson, "Antitrust Policy in Transition, "*Mississippi Valley Historical Review,* XLVIII (1961).

14. See, for example, Robert H. Wiebe, *Businessmen and Reform: A Study of the Progressive Movement* (Cambridge, Mass., Harvard University Press, 1962).

15. George E. Mowry, *The Era of Theodore Roosevelt 1900–1912* (New York, Harper & Bros., 1958) pp. 220–24.

16. Horace Samuel Merrill and Marion Galbraith Merrill, *The Republican Command 1897–1913* (Lexington, Ky., The University of Kentucky Press, 1971), p. 242.

17. George E. Mowry, *The California Progressives* (Berkeley, University of California Press, 1951, p. 90.

18. *The Life and Times of Theodore Roosevelt,* p. 414.

Horace Samuel Merrill (Pages 125–132)

1. Horace Samuel Merrill and Marion Galbraith Merrill, *The Republican Command, 1897–1913* (Lexington: The University Press of Kentucky, 1971), pp. 4, 16–35, 93–94, 144, 146, 159, 243–245.

2. Roosevelt to Taft, March 19, 1903, Theodore Roosevelt Papers, Manuscripts Division, Library of Congress.

3. Merrill and Merrill, *Republican Command,* pp. 216–218, 243.

4. *Ibid.,* pp. 225–226.

5. *Ibid.,* p. 202.

6. *Ibid.,* pp. 38, 91, 97, 122–123.

7. Roosevelt to Taft, July 15, 1901, Roosevelt papers.

8. John Morton Blum, *The Republican Roosevelt* (Cambridge: Harvard University Press, 1954), pp. 75–78.

9. Merrill and Merrill, *Republican Command,* pp. 147–148, 157–158.

10. Henry L. Higginson to Roosevelt, November 6, 1903, Roosevelt Papers.

11. Merrill and Merrill, *Republican Command,* p. 157.

12. Roosevelt to John Byrne, December 29, 1903, Roosevelt Papers.

13. James D. Richardson, *A Compilation of the Messages and Papers of the Presidents* (New York: Bureau of National Literature Incorporated, 20 vols. 1897–1927), 14: 6787.

14. Merrill and Merrill, *Republican Command,* pp. 268–269.

Charles T. Morrissey (Pages 133–158)

1. Thomas A. Bailey, *Presidential Greatness: The Image and The Man From George Washington to the Present* (New York: Appleton-Century, 1966), p. 111.

The citations which follow are references solely to *un*published sources. Where the text of this essay does not indicate a footnote the information is drawn from published material—diaries such as those of Harold L. Ickes and David E. Lilienthal, memoirs such as those of Samuel I. Rosenman and Donald R. Richberg, or newspaper and magazine articles, the *Congressional Record*, transcripts of press conferences, histories of the period, etc. An early draft of this essay showed that 130 citations would be necessary to document every statement; the decision to restrict footnotes to unpublished items was made in the interest of space and the patience of the general reader. As noted in the bibliographic essay, the entire story of the third-term issue in American political history is lively and often unexplored, and accordingly the author welcomes inquiry from readers who wish to pursue particular interests.

2. Irving Fisher to Franklin D. Roosevelt, February 6, 1940, in President's Personal File 431, Roosevelt Papers, Franklin D. Roosevelt Library, Hyde Park, New York.

3. Max Askotzky to Franklin D. Roosevelt, March 13, 1940, in Official File 2526, Roosevelt Papers.

4. Maury Maverick to Franklin D. Roosevelt, January 15, 1940, in President's Personal File 3446, Roosevelt Papers. Maverick's letter about the "Saint of the Impossible," July 10, 1936, is in the same file.

5. Leon B. Sittenfeld to Franklin D. Roosevelt, December 9, 1939, in Official File 2526, Roosevelt Papers.

6. Henry C. Bates, "Antecedents of the 1940 Democratic National Convention," (M.A. thesis, Columbia University, 1952), p. 3.

7. M. M. Harper to William E. Borah, December 16, 1939, in "Political, Third Term" folder, Borah Papers, Manuscripts Division, Library of Congress, Washington, D. C.

8. Jesse H. Jones to James A. Farley, March 10, 1948, in Jones Papers, Manuscripts Division, Library of Congress.

9. *The Reminiscences of Arthur Krock*, Part I (1950), p. 51, in the Oral History Collection of Columbia University, New York.

10. Rayburn's remark was to this author, Washington, D. C., March 8, 1961. The second quotation was attributed to Marguerite Le Hand and conveyed by a former White House staff-member, who requested nonattribution, in an interview with me in Washington, D. C., April 22, 1965.

11. Joseph F. Guffey, *Seventy Years on the Red-Fire Wagon: From Tilden to Truman Through New Freedom and New Deal* (privately printed, 1952), p. 122.

12. Herbert Maw to Franklin D. Roosevelt, July 17, 1943; Roosevelt to Maw, October 8, 1943, both in President's Personal File 7348, Roosevelt Papers.

13. Since more than one participant in the Tarrytown Conference on Six Empire State Presidents went searching for this quotation in Mr. Lubell's well-known books and reported he could not find it, note here that it appears in Lubell's article, "Post-Mortem: Who Elected Roosevelt?" in the *Saturday Evening Post*, Volume 213, Number 4 (January 25, 1941), p. 94.

SELECTED BIBLIOGRAPHY

Empire State Presidents
and their Contemporaries

Selected Bibliography

Alexander, Holmes M. *The American Talleyrand; The Career and Contemporaries of Martin Van Buren, Eighth President* (New York, Harper, 1935). Reprinted in New York by Russell & Russell (1968).

Beale, Howard K. *Theodore Roosevelt and the Rise of America to World Power* (Baltimore: The Johns Hopkins Press, 1956).

Black, Gilbert J. *Theodore Roosevelt, 1858-1919: Chronology-Documents-Bibliographical Aids.* (Dobbs Ferry, N. Y.: Oceana Publications, 1969).

Blum, John N. *The Republican Roosevelt* (Cambridge, Mass.: Harvard University Press, 1954).

Bremner, Howard F. *Franklin D. Roosevelt, 1882–1945: Chronology-Documents-Bibliographical Aids* (Dobbs Ferry, N. Y.: Oceana Publications, 1971).

Burns, James MacGregor. *Roosevelt: The Lion and the Fox* (New York: Harcourt, Brace, 1956).

Burns, James MacGregor. *Roosevelt: The Soldier of Freedom* (New York: Harcourt Brace Jovanovich, 1970).

Burton, David H. *Theodore Roosevelt* (New York: Twayne, 1972).

Chessman, G. Wallace. *Theodore Roosevelt and the Politics of Power* (Boston: Little, Brown & Co., 1969).

Curtis, James C. *The Fox at Bay: Martin Van Buren and the Presidency, 1837–1841* (Lexington: University Press of Kentucky, 1970).

Davis, Kenneth S. *FDR: The Beckoning of Destiny, 1882–1928; A History* (New York: Putnam, 1972).

Davison, Kenneth E. *The Presidency of Rutherford B. Hayes* (Westport, Conn.: Greenwood Press, 1972).

De Santis, Vincent P. *Republicans Face the Southern Question: The New Departure Years, 1877–1897* (Baltimore: Johns Hopkins Press, 1959). Reprinted in New York by Greenwood Press (1969).

The Era of Franklin D. Roosevelt: A Selected Bibliography of Periodical and Dissertation Literature, compiled and annotated by William J. Stewart (Hyde Park, N. Y.: General Services Administration for the Franklin D. Roosevelt Library, 1967).

Farrell, John J. *Zachary Taylor, 1784–1850–Millard Fillmore, 1800–1874: Chronology-Documents-Bibliographical Aids* (Dobbs Ferry, N. Y.: Oceana Publications, 1971).

Furer, Howard B. *James A. Garfield, 1831–1881–Chester A. Arthur, 1830–1886: Chronology-Documents-Bibliographical Aids* (Dobbs Ferry, N. Y.: Oceana Publications, 1970).

Grantham, Dewey, ed. *Theodore Roosevelt: Great Lives Observed* (Englewood Cliffs, N. J.: Prentice-Hall, 1971).

Hamilton, Holman. *Prologue to Conflicts: The Crisis and Compromise of 1850* (Lexington: University Press of Kentucky, 1964).

Harbaugh, William H. *Power and Responsibility; The Life and Times of Theodore Roosevelt* (New York: Farrar, Straus and Cudahy, 1961). A revision was published in paperback under the title *The Life and Times of Theodore Roosevelt* (New York: Collier Books, 1963).

Hirsch, Mark D. *William C. Whitney, Modern Warwick* (New York: Dodd, Mead, 1948). Reprinted in Hamden, Conn., by Archon Books (1969).

Hollingsworth, Joseph R. *The Whirligig of Politics: The Democracy of Cleveland and Bryan* (Chicago: University of Chicago Press, 1963).

Howe, George Frederick. *Chester A. Arthur: A Quarter-Century of Machine Politics* (New York: Dodd, Mead, 1934). Reprinted in New York by F. Ungar (1957).

Kirwin, Albwert D. *John J. Crittenden: The Struggle for the Union* (Lexington: University Press of Kentucky, 1962).

Koenig, Louis W. *Bryan: A Political Biography of William Jennings Bryan* (New York: Putnam, 1971).

Koenig, Louis W. *The Chief Executive*, rev. ed. (New York: Harcourt, Brace & World, 1968).

Leuchtenburg, William E. *Franklin D. Roosevelt and the New Deal, 1932–1940* (New York: Harper & Row, 1963).

McCormick, Richard P. *The Second American Party System: Party Formation in the Jacksonian Era* (Chapel Hill: University of North Carolina Press, 1966).

McCoy, Donald R. *Angry Voices: Left-of-Center Politics in the New Deal Era* (Lawrence: University of Kansas Press, 1958). Reprinted in Port Washington, N. Y., by Kennikat Press (1971).

Merrill, Horace S. *Bourbon Democracy of the Middle West, 1865–1896.* (Baton Rouge: Louisiana State University Press, 1953). Reprinted with a new introduction in Seattle by the University of Washington Press (1967).

Merrill, Horace S. *Bourbon Leader: Grover Cleveland and the Democratic Party* (Boston: Little, Brown & Co., 1957).

Merrill, Horace S., and Marion G. Merrill. *The Republican Command, 1897–1913* (Lexington: University Press of Kentucky, 1971).

Moscow, Warren. *Roosevelt and Willkie* (Englewood Cliffs, N. J.: Prentice-Hall, 1968).

Mowry, George E. *The Era of Theodore Roosevelt* (New York: Harper & Brothers, 1958).

Nevins, Allan. *Grover Cleveland: A Study in Courage* (New York: Dodd, Mead, 1932).

Parmet, Herbert S., and Marie B. Hecht. *Never Again, A President Runs For a Third Term* (New York: Macmillan, 1968).

Pessen, Edward. *Jacksonian America: Society, Personality, and Politics.* (Homewood, Ill.: Dorsey Press, 1969).

The Presidents of the United States, 1789–1962, compiled by Donald H. Mugridge (Washington: Library of Congress, 1963).

Pringle, Henry F. *Theodore Roosevelt: A Biography* (New York: Harcourt, Brace, 1931).

Rayback, Robert J. *Millard Fillmore; Biography of a President*

(Buffalo: published for the Buffalo Historical Society by H. Stewart, 1959).

Remini, Robert V. *Martin Van Buren and the Making of the Democratic Party* (New York: Columbia University Press, 1959).

Sievers, Harry J. *Benjamin Harrison*, 3 vols. (Indianapolis: Bobbs-Merrill Co., 1952–[68]).

Sloan, Irving J. *Martin Van Buren, 1782–1862: Chronology-Documents-Bibliographical Aids* (Dobbs Ferry, N. Y.: Oceana Publications, 1969).

Snyder, Charles M. *The Jacksonian Heritage; Pennsylvania Politics, 1833–1848* (Harrisburg: Pennsylvania Historical and Museum Commission, 1958).

Tugwell, Rexford G. *Grover Cleveland* (New York: Macmillan, 1968).

Tugwell, Rexford G. *In Search of Roosevelt* (Cambridge, Mass.: Harvard University Press, 1972).

Vexler, Robert J. *Grover Cleveland, 1837–1908: Chronology-Documents-Bibliographical Aids* (Dobbs Ferry, N. Y.: Oceana Publications, 1968).

CONTRIBUTORS

CONTRIBUTORS

KENNETH E. DAVISON is Professor of History and American Studies and Chairman of the Department of American Studies at Heidelberg College in Tiffin, Ohio. He received his advanced degrees from Western Reserve University. His most recent publication, *The Presidency of Rutherford B. Hayes*, received the Ohioana Library Association's prize for the best history book of 1972. Recently he was designated editor of the Public Papers of Rutherford B. Hayes, the publication of which is in progress. He is also at work on a comprehensive bibliography of the American presidency.

VINCENT P. DE SANTIS is Professor of History at the University of Notre Dame and was Chairman of the Department from 1963 to 1971. Among his many publications on the history of the United States since 1865 are *Republicans Face the Southern Question; The Shaping of Modern America 1877–1916; The Gilded Age— A Bibliography;* and *America Past and Present.* His articles have appeared in such periodicals as *Journal of Negro History, Review of Politics, Journal of Southern History, Current History, Indiana Magazine of History, Mid-America,* and *Catholic Historical Review.* He has been awarded a Guggenheim Fellowship, a Fulbright Professorship in Italy, a Research Grant from the Henry E. Huntington Library, and American Philosophical Society Awards.

WILLIAM H. HARBAUGH has been Professor of History at the University of Virginia since 1966. A native of New Jersey, he received his advanced degrees from Columbia and Northwestern, and taught previously at Bucknell, Rutgers, and the Universities of Connecticut and Maryland. Dr. Harbaugh is the author of *Power and Responsibility: The Life and Times of Theodore Roosevelt* and of *Lawyer's Lawyer: The Life of John W. Davis.* He is also the editor of *The Writings of Theodore Roosevelt* and is a contributor to *History of American Presidential Elections* and *History of U. S. Political Parties.*

MARK D. HIRSCH is Chairman of the History Department at Bronx Community College of the City University of New York. He has also taught graduate and elective courses at Columbia

University, Yale University, and Long Island University and at
the City College. A native New Yorker, he received his advanced
degrees from Columbia University. Among his many publications, mainly on New York City and State history, is a biography,
William C. Whitney, Modern Warwick. He is a History Consult-
ant to the National Endowment for the Humanities and a member of the Board of Editors for the New York State Historical
Association.

Louis W. Koenig is Professor of Government at New York University, after having been in Washington with the State Department, the foreign affairs task force of the First Hoover Commission, and the Bureau of the Budget. His books include *The
Chief Executive, The Invisible Presidency*, and *The Presidency
Today*, with Edward S. Corwin. He edited *The Truman Administration*, and his most recent book is *Bryan: A Political Biography of William Jennings Bryan*. Articles by Professor Koenig
have appeared in *American Heritage, The Nation, Saturday
Review, The Virginia Quarterly*, and the *New York Times Magazine*.

Richard P. McCormick is Professor of History and University
Historian at Rutgers University. A specialist in American political history, he is the author of *The Second American Party System: Party Formation in the Jacksonian Era* and numerous other
books and articles. In 1961–62 he was a visiting professor at
Cambridge University, and in 1972 he delivered the Commonwealth Lecture at the University of London. He is a member of
the Executive Board of the Organization of American Historians
and the American Revolution Bicentennial Commission.

Donald R. McCoy is Professor of American History at the University of Kansas. He was educated at the University of Denver
and took graduate degrees in history from the University of Chicago and the American University, and has been a member of
the staff of the National Archives and of the Harry S. Truman
Library Institute. He has also taught at the State University of
New York (Cortland) and the University of Bonn. In addition
to numerous articles, he is the author of monographs on radical-
ism during the 1930s and (with R. T. Ruetten) on the Truman

Administration and minority rights, and of biographies of Calvin Coolidge and Alfred Landon. His book-length essay on the United States between the world wars, entitled *Coming of Age*, was recently published.

HORACE SAMUEL MERRILL is Professor of History at the University of Maryland. A native of Wisconsin, he received his advanced degrees at the University of Wisconsin. His most recent publication, *The Republican Command, 1897–1913*, written with his wife, Marion Galbraith Merrill, was awarded the 1972 Phi Alpha Theta Book Award for the best book published by a member of the Society in the field of history. He is also the author of *Bourbon Democracy of the Middle West, 1865–1896; Bourbon Leader: Grover Cleveland and the Democratic Party;* and *William Freeman Vilas, Doctrinaire Democrat.*

CHARLES T. MORRISSEY is Director of the Vermont Historical Society and Research Professor of History at Dartmouth College, where he also directs the Dartmouth College Oral History Project. He holds degrees in history from Dartmouth College and the University of California at Berkeley. From 1971 to 1973 he was on leave to direct the Ford Foundation Oral History Project in New York City. His other oral history activities include being Oral Historian for the Harry S. Truman Library, Chief of the John F. Kennedy Library Oral History Project, Director of the Christian A. Herter Oral History Project at Harvard University, and interviewing for projects on Herbert Hoover and on Eugene McCarthy's 1968 campaign for the Democratic Nomination. He was Vice-president of the Oral History Association in 1970–71, and President in 1971–72. He is the author of a dozen articles on oral history and the history of the American presidency.

EDWARD PESSEN is Distinguished Professor of History at Baruch College and the Graduate Center of the City University of New York. He is the author of *Riches, Class, and Power Before the Civil War; Jacksonian America: Society, Personality, and Politics; New Perspectives on Jacksonian Parties and Politics; Most Uncommon Jacksonians;* and the essay on United States History 1816–1850 in the most recent edition of *Encyclopaedia Britannica.* Scheduled for publication are his *Three Centuries of Social*

Mobility in America, and *Jacksonian Society: A Documentary Portrait,* a volume in the Bobbs-Merrill *American Heritage* Series. He is presently writing a comprehensive text in American History and two interpretive books on nineteenth-century society.

ROBERT J. RAYBACK teaches history at Syracuse University. He studied at Western Reserve University and received his advanced degrees from the University of Wisconsin. He has published several works on nineteenth-century America, including a biography of Millard Fillmore. He has also edited and contributed to *Richards Atlas of New York* and is coauthor of *History of Our United States.*

THOMAS C. REEVES is Professor of History at the University of Wisconsin-Parkside. A native of Tacoma, Washington, he studied at the University of California, Santa Barbara. His biography of Chester Alan Arthur, *The Gentleman Boss,* is scheduled for publication in 1974. Among his other works are *Freedom and the Foundation: The Fund for the Republic in the Era of McCarthyism,* and, as editor, *Foundations under Fire* and *McCarthyism.* He has published many articles on American history since 1877, particularly in the fields of politics and civil liberties.

CHARLES M. SNYDER was Professor of History at the State University of New York at Oswego, until his retirement in 1972. He received his M.A. degree from Bucknell University and his Ph.D. from the University of Pennsylvania. Among his publications are *The Jacksonian Heritage: Pennsylvania Politics, 1833–1848; Dr. Mary Walker, The Little Lady in Pants;* and *Owsego: From Buckskin to Bustles.* He has contributed articles to numerous periodicals, including *New York History, Southwestern Historical Quarterly, American Archivist, Vermont History,* and *California Historian.*

Editor

HARRY J. SIEVERS, S. J. is Dean of the Graduate School of Arts and Sciences and Dean of the Liberal Arts Faculty at Rose Hill, Fordham University. He is a former Chairman of the History Department at Fordham and also taught at Canisius College, Georgetown University, and Bellarmine College in Plattsburgh, N.Y. Among his many works concerning the presidency is a three-volume biography of Benjamin Harrison. The third and final volume is *Benjamin Harrison: Hoosier President, The White House & After, 1889–1901.* He is also editor of *William McKinley, 1843–1901.*

INDEX

INDEX

Sleepy Hollow Restorations, Incorporated, is a nonprofit educational institution chartered by the State of New York. Established under an endowment provided by the late John D. Rockefeller, Jr., it owns and maintains Van Cortlandt Manor, in Croton-on-Hudson, a distinguished eighteenth-century family residence, and Sunnyside, Washington Irving's picturesque home in Tarrytown. Recently, Sleepy Hollow Restorations completed the reconstruction of Philipsburg Manor, Upper Mills, at its original site on the Pocantico River, an impressive example of a colonial commercial-mill complex.